imperialism
without colonies

imperialism without colonies

HARRY MAGDOFF

MONTHLY REVIEW PRESS

New York

Library of Congress Cataloging-in-Publication Data
is available from the publisher.

ISBN 1-58367-094-7 paperback

Monthly Review Press
122 West 27th Street
New York, NY 10001

10 9 8 7 6 5 4 3 2 1

Manufactured in Canada

Contents

9 | INTRODUCTION by John Bellamy Foster

20 | 1. The Achievement of Paul Baran

35 | 2. The New Imperialism

67 | 3. The American Empire and the U.S. Economy

91 | 4. Imperialism Without Colonies

114 | 5. Militarism and Imperialism

124 | 6. The Limits of International Economic Reform

133 | NOTES

145 | INDEX

Editorial Note

THE ESSAYS IN THIS VOLUME were first published between 1965 and 1978. They have been selected in order to give a clear overview of Harry Magdoff's seminal work on imperialism and for their relevance to understanding the essential forces at work in reshaping imperialism today, in the early twenty-first century.

CHAPTER 1, "The Achievement of Paul Baran," was first published in *Monthly Review*, March 1965, in a special issue dedicated to Baran's memory. The special issue was later republished as Paul M. Sweezy and Leo Huberman, ed., *Paul Baran: A Collective Portrait* (New York: Monthly Review Press, 1965). In giving an account of Baran's achievement, the chapter at the same time describes the economic foundations on which Magdoff's account of imperialism was built and sets out and defends the socialist values that informed the work of both of them, and the *Monthly Review* project to which they devoted themselves.

CHAPTER 2, "The Age of Imperialism," was first published in *Monthly Review*, June 1968, and became the title-essay of Magdoff's book, *The Age of Imperialism* (New York: Monthly Review Press, 1969). It is the fullest single account in Magdoff's work of the nature of imperialism in the period after 1945 and gives a comprehensive and detailed overview of its economic mechanisms.

CHAPTER 3, "The American Empire and the U.S. Economy," began life as a paper delivered at the Socialist Scholars Conference in September 1966, was published in *Monthly Review*, November 1966, and again as the concluding chapter of *The Age of Imperialism*. It analyzes the essential role of imperialism for sustaining U.S. capitalism and demonstrates the leading role of the United States in imperialism since 1945.

CHAPTER 4, "Imperialism Without Colonies" was originally presented at a seminar at Oxford University in 1970, was first published in Roger Owen and Robert Sutcliffe, ed., *Studies in the Theory of Imperialism* (London: Longmans, 1972), and included in Harry Magdoff, *Imperialism: From the Colonial Age to the Present* (New York: Monthly Review Press, 1976). It locates modern imperialism within the longer history of imperialism, demonstrating continuities and changes within that history and examining the economic bases of imperialism after the end of colonialism.

CHAPTER 5, "Militarism and Imperialism" was originally presented at the Annual Meeting of the American Economic Association in December 1969, was first published in Monthly Review, February 1970, and included in *Imperialism: From the Colonial Age to the Present*. It makes clear the importance of military aggression (and military spending) in sustaining the global capitalist system, showing how the capitalist system itself brings war in its wake.

CHAPTER 6, "The Limits of International Reform" was published in *Monthly Review*, May 1978. Most of Magdoff's writings on imperialism focus on the mechanisms through which imperialist countries dominate and exploit the Third World. This piece completes the picture by examining the strategies of resistance of Third World leaders calling for a new international economic order and exposing the illusion that a new division of global wealth and income can be created within the capitalist global order.

Editorial changes have been kept to a minimum throughout. We have corrected typographical errors, filled in incomplete references, renumbered tables for consistency, and brought some aspects of the text into conformity with the current *Chicago Manual of Style*.

Although these essays were written over a decade or more, it will be clear to the reader that all of them belong to a single, integrated project. They form a coherent whole, illuminating the time in which they were written and our own time as well. This volume is published to honor Harry Magdoff on the occasion of his ninetieth birthday, and also to provide a weapon in the struggle for a better world.

JOHN BELLAMY FOSTER # Introduction

ON NOVEMBER 11, 2000, Richard Haass—a member of the National Security Council and special assistant to the president under the elder Bush, soon to be appointed director of policy planning in the state department of newly elected President George W. Bush—delivered a paper in Atlanta entitled "Imperial America." For the United States to succeed at its objective of global preeminence, he declared, it would be necessary for Americans to "re-conceive their role from a traditional nation-state to an imperial power." Haass eschewed the term "imperialist" in describing America's role, preferring "imperial," since the former connoted "exploitation, normally for commercial ends," and "territorial control." Nevertheless, the intent was perfectly clear:

> To advocate an imperial foreign policy is to call for a foreign policy that attempts to organize the world along certain principles affecting relations between states and conditions within them. The U.S. role would resemble 19th century Great Britain….Coercion and the use of force would normally be a last resort; what was written by John Gallagher and Ronald Robinson about Britain a century and a half ago, that "The British policy followed the principle of extending control informally if possible and formally if necessary," could be applied to the American role at the start of the new century.[1]

The existence of an American empire is no secret. It is widely, even universally, recognized in most parts of the world, though traditionally denied by the powers that be in the United States. What Haass was calling for, however, was a much more open acknowledgement of this imperial role by Washington, in full view of the American population and the world, in order to further Washington's imperial ambitions. "The fundamental question that continues to confront American foreign policy," he explained, "is what to do with a surplus of power and the many and considerable advantages this surplus confers on the United States." This surplus of power could only be put to use by recognizing that United States had imperial interests on the scale of Britain in the nineteenth century. The world should therefore be given notice that Washington was prepared to "extend its control," informally if possible and formally if not, to secure what it considered to be its legitimate interests across the face of the globe. The final section of Haass' paper carried the heading "Imperialism Begins at Home." It concluded: "the greater risk facing the United States at this juncture...is that it will squander the opportunity to bring about a world supportive of its core interests by doing too little. Imperial understretch, not overstretch, appears the greater danger of the two."

There is every reason to believe that the "Imperial America" argument espoused by Haass represents in broad outline the now dominant view of the U.S. ruling class, together with the U.S. state that primarily serves that class. After many years of denying the existence of U.S. empire, received opinion in the United States has now adopted a position that glories in the "American imperium," with its "imperial military," and "imperial protectorates."[2] This shift in external posture first occurred at the end of the 1990s, when it became apparent that not only was the United States the sole remaining superpower following the demise of the Soviet Union, but also that Europe and Japan, due to slowdowns in their rates of economic growth relative to that of the United States, were now less able to rival it economically. Nor did Europe seem to be able to act militarily without the United States even within its own region, in relation to the debacle of the Yugoslavian civil wars.

After Washington launched its global War on Terrorism, following September 11, 2001, the imperial dimensions of U.S. foreign policy were increasingly obvious. U.S. empire is therefore now portrayed by political pundits and the mainstream media as a necessary "burden" falling on the United States as a result its unparalleled role on the world stage. The United States is said to be at the head of a new kind of empire, divorced from national interest, economic exploitation, racism, or colonialism, and that exists only to promote freedom and human rights. As Michael Ignatieff, Professor of Human Rights Policy at the Kennedy School of Government, Harvard University, proclaimed in the *New York Times Magazine* (January 5, 2003), "America's empire is not like empires of times past, built on colonies, conquest and the white man's burden....The 21st century imperium is a new invention in the annals of political science, an empire lite, a global hegemony whose grace notes are free markets, human rights and democracy, enforced by the most awesome military power the world has ever known."[3]

Such high-sounding words aside, what makes this "21st century imperium" an overriding concern for humanity today is Washington's increased readiness to use its unrivaled military power to invade and occupy other countries whenever it deems this absolutely necessary to achieve its ends. Yet, as Indian economist Prabhat Patnaik observed more than a decade ago, "No Marxist ever derived the existence of imperialism from the fact of wars; on the contrary the existence of wars was explained in terms of imperialism."[4] Once the reality of imperialism has been brought back to the forefront of world attention as a result of such wars it is important to search out its underlying causes.

Classic Imperialism

ONE OF THE MOST influential mainstream historical accounts of British imperialism in the nineteenth century was presented in an article entitled "The Imperialism of Free Trade," written a half-century ago by economic historians John Gallagher and Ronald Robinson. A part of this analysis was utilized by Haass to advance his "Imperial America" argument. Gallagher and Robinson's central thesis in their article was simple: *imperialism is a continuous reality of economic expansion in modern times.* Those who associated imperialism primarily with colonies and colonialism, and who therefore took the scramble for Africa and late nineteenth century *colonial* expansion as the basis for a general model of imperialism, were wrong. British imperialism throughout the nineteenth century remained essentially the same in its inner logic despite the concentration on expanding free trade in one period and on annexing colonies in another. As Gallagher and Robinson elaborated (in the same passage from which Haass quoted):

> British policy followed the principle of extending control informally if possible and formally if necessary. To label the one method 'anti-imperialist' and the other 'imperialist,' is to ignore the fact that whatever the method British interests were steadily safeguarded and extended. The usual summing up of the policy of the free trade empire as 'trade not rule' should read 'trade with informal control if possible; trade with rule when necessary.'…Despite…attempts at 'imperialism on the cheap,' the foreign challenges to British paramountcy in tropical Africa [in the late nineteenth century] and the comparative absence there of large-scale, strong, indigenous political organizations which had served informal expansion so well elsewhere, eventually dictated the switch to formal rule.[5]

For those seeking to comprehend British imperialism in the nineteenth century, this argument suggested, it is the "imperialism of free trade" and not colonialism that should be the primary focus. Only when the economic ends of Britain could not be secured by informal control did it resort to formal imperialism or colonization—that is, direct and continuing use of military and political control—to achieve its ends. If it has often been said that "trade followed the flag," it would be far more correct to say that there was "a general tendency for British trade to follow the invisible flag of informal empire." The "distinctive feature" of the "British imperialism of free trade in the nineteenth century," these authors argued, was that its use of its military force and hegemonic power in general was primarily limited to establishing secure conditions for economic dominance and expansion.

The clearest example of such informal imperialism was the British role in South America in the nineteenth century. Britain maintained its control in the region through various commercial treaties and financial relationships backed by British sea power. As British Foreign Minister George Canning put it in 1824: "Spanish America is free; and if we do not mismanage our affairs sadly she is *English.*"[6] At all times, Gallagher and Robinson state, British influence was exercised so as to convert such "areas into complementary satellite economies, which would provide raw materials and food for Great Britain, and provide widening markets for its manufactures." When left with no other way of enforcing its dominance, Britain was always ready to resort to active interventions—as it did repeatedly in Latin America in the nineteenth century.

As the distinguished German historian Wolfgang J. Mommsen noted in his *Theories of Imperialism,* the significance of this concept of informal imperialism was that it tended to bridge the gap between non-Marxist and Marxist approaches, since it stressed the historical continuity of imperialism as a manifestation of economic expansion (not confusing it simply with its more formal political-military occurrences):

> By recognizing that there are numerous informal types of imperialist domination which precede or accompany the establishment of formal rule, or even make it unnecessary, Western [non-Marxist] thinking on the subject of imperialism has drawn closer to Marxist theory....Generally speaking, most non-Marxist theoreticians admit nowadays that dependency of an imperialist sort may well result from the most varied kinds of informal influence, especially of an economic nature. Imperialist forces at the colonial periphery were by no means obliged constantly to resort to the actual use of political power: it was generally quite enough

to know that the imperialist groups could count on support from the metropolitan power in the event of a crisis. Formal political rule thus appears only as the most specific, but not the normal type of imperialist development.[7]

Ironically, Gallagher and Robinson distinguished their approach from the classic accounts of John Hobson (in his 1902 *Imperialism: A Study*) and Lenin (in his 1916 *Imperialism, the Highest Stage of Capitalism*) by associating both Hobson's and Lenin's views with a narrower spectrum of cases involving formal control or colonialism. By identifying the last quarter of the nineteenth century, when colonial annexations were at their height, as a qualitatively new stage of capitalism—the monopoly or imperialist stage, Lenin in particular, these authors argued, had come to associate imperialism with formal rather than informal control.

However, this criticism fell wide of the mark, since Lenin himself had emphasized that imperialism did not necessarily involve formal control, as witnessed especially by British imperialism in Latin America in the nineteenth century. "The division of the world into...colony-owning countries on the one hand and colonies on the other," he observed, did not exhaust the core-periphery relations between nations states. Indeed Lenin pointed to "a variety of forms of dependent countries; countries, which, officially, are politically independent, but which are, in fact, enmeshed in the net of financial and diplomatic dependence...the semi-colony," including cases like Argentina, which was so dependent financially on London that it was a virtual colony.[8]

The reality of an informal imperialism of free trade (or imperialism without colonies) was never an enigma to Marxist theory, which viewed imperialism as a historical process associated with capitalist expansion—only secondarily affected by the particular political forms in which it manifested itself. The reason for characterizing the last quarter of the nineteenth century as the imperialist *stage* in the work of Lenin and most subsequent Marxist theorists, did not have to do mainly with a shift from informal to formal imperialism, or the mere fact of widespread annexations within the periphery, but rather with the evolution of capitalism itself, which had developed into its *monopoly* stage, creating a qualitatively new type of imperialism. It was this historically specific analysis of imperialism as a manifestation of capitalist development in all of its complexity (economic/political/military—core and periphery) that was to give the Marxist theory of imperialism its importance as a coherent way of understanding the deeper globalizing tendencies of the system.

In this interpretation, there was a sense in which imperialism was inherent in capitalism from the beginning. Many of the features of contemporary imperialism, such as the development of the world market, the division between core and periphery, the competitive hunt for colonies or semi-colonies, the extraction of surplus, the securing of raw materials to bring back to the mother country, etc. are part of capitalism as a global system from the late fifteenth century on. Imperialism, in the widest sense, had its sources in the accumulation dynamic of the system (as basic as the pursuit of profits itself), which encouraged the countries at the center of the capitalist world economy, and particularly the wealthy interests within these countries, to feather their own nests by appropriating surplus and vital resources from the periphery—what Pierre Jalée called *The Pillage of the Third World*.[9] By a variety of coercive means, the poorer satellite economies were so structured—beginning in the age of conquest in the late fifteenth and sixteenth centuries—that their systems of production and distribution served not so much their own needs as those of the dominant metropoles. Nevertheless, the recognition of such commonalities in imperialism in the various phases of capitalist development was entirely consistent with the observation that there had been a qualitative change in the nature and significance of imperialism that commenced in the last quarter of the nineteenth century, sufficient to cause Lenin to associate this with a new stage of capitalism.

Marxists have therefore often distinguished between an older imperialism and what was called the "new imperialism" that began in the final decades of the nineteenth century. What distinguished this new imperialism was primarily two things: 1) the breakdown of British hegemony and increased competition for control over global territories between the various advanced capitalist states; 2) the rise of monopolistic corporations—large, integrated industrial and financial firms—as the dominant economic actors in all of the advanced capitalist states. The new mammoth corporations by their very nature sought to expand beyond national bounds and dominate global production and consumption. As Harry Magdoff observes in this book, "The urge to dominate is integral to business." Monopolistic firms engaged in this imperial struggle were frequently favored by their own nation states. The Marxist theory of the new imperialism, with its focus on the rise of the giant firms, thus pointed to the changed global economic circumstances that were to emerge along with what later came to be known as multinational or global corporations. All of this became the context in which older phenomena, such as the extraction of surplus, the race for control of raw materials and resources, the creation of economic dependencies in the global periphery and the unending contest among rival capitalist powers, manifested themselves in new and transformed ways.

It was this understanding of imperialism as a historical reality of capitalist development, one that took on new characteristics as the system itself evolved that most sharply separated the Marxist approach from mainstream interpretations. The latter frequently saw imperialism as a mere policy and associated it primarily with political and military actions on the part of states. In the more widely disseminated mainstream view (from which realist economic historians like Gallagher and Robinson dissented), imperialism was present only in overt instances of political and territorial control ushered in by actual military conquest. In the contrasting Marxist view, imperialism occurred not simply through the policies of states but also through the actions of corporations and the mechanisms of trade, finance and investment. It involved a whole constellation of class relations, including the nurturing of local collaborators or comprador elements in the dependent societies. Any explanation of how imperialism worked thus necessitated a description of an entire system or monopoly capitalism. Informal control of countries on the periphery of the capitalist world system by countries at the center of the system was as important, in this view, as formal control. Struggles over hegemony and more generally rivalries among the leading capitalist states were continuous, but took on changing forms depending on the economic, political and military resources at their disposal.

Imperial America in the Post-Cold War World

IF THE MAIN distinguishing feature of modern imperialism, in the Marxist view, was associated with the rise to dominance of the giant corporations, the ordering of power within the system, as reflected in the relative position of various nation states, nonetheless shifted considerably over time. In the late nineteenth and early twentieth century the principal global reality was the decline in British hegemony and the increased rivalry among the advanced capitalist states that followed, leading to the First and Second World Wars. The rise of the Soviet Union in the context of the First World War posed an external challenge to the system eventually leading to a Cold War struggle between the United States, the new hegemonic power of the capitalist world economy following the Second World War, and the Soviet Union. The fall of the latter in 1991 left the

United States as the sole superpower. By the end of the 1990s the United States had gained on its main economic rivals as well. The result of all of this by the beginning of the new century, as Henry Kissinger declared in 2001 in *Does America Need a Foreign Policy?*, was that the U.S. had achieved "a pre-eminence not enjoyed by even the greatest empires of the past."[10]

This naturally led to the question: what was the United States to do with its enormous "surplus of power"? The answer of Washington, particularly after 9-11, has been to pursue its imperial ambitions through renewed interventions in the global periphery—on a scale not seen since the Vietnam War. In the waging of its imperial War on Terrorism the U.S. state is at one with the expansionary goals of U.S. business. As *Business Week Online* in late January 2003 expressed the economic benefits to be derived from a U.S. invasion of Iraq: "Since the U.S. military would control Iraq's oil and gas deposits [the second largest known reserves in the world after Saudi Arabia] for some time, U.S. companies could be in line for a lucrative slice of the business. They may snag drilling rights too." Companies in the oil service industry, which is dominated by the United States, might "feel just as victorious as the U.S. Special Forces."[11] Indeed, the main object of such military invasions is regime change and the subsequent restructuring of the economy of the "rogue state"—so-called because outside the imperial order defined primarily by the United States—to make it conform to the dominant requirements of the capitalist world economy, which includes opening up its resources to more extensive exploitation.

Richard Haass (whose responsibilities in the present administration were extended to include that of U.S. Coordinator of policy towards the future of Afghanistan) pointed out in his book *Intervention*, that regime change often can only be accomplished through a full-scale military invasion leaving the conquered nation in ruins and necessitating subsequent "nation-building":

> It is difficult to target specific individuals with military force....U.S. efforts to use force to bring about changes in political leadership failed in the cases of Qaddafi in Libya, Saddam in Iraq, and Aideed in Somalia. Force can create a context in which political change is more likely, but without extraordinary intelligence and more than a little good fortune, force by itself is unlikely to bring about specific political changes. The only way to increase the likelihood of such change is through highly intrusive forms of intervention, such as nation-building, which involves first eliminating all opposition and then engaging in an occupation that allows for substantial engineering of another society.[12]

Such a "nation-building" occupation, Haass stressed, involves "defeating and disarming any local opposition and establishing a political authority that enjoys a monopoly or near-monopoly of control over the legitimate use of force." (This is Max Weber's well-known definition of a state—though imposed in this case by an invading force from outside.) It therefore requires, as Haass observed quoting one foreign policy analyst, an occupation of "imperial proportions and possibly of endless duration."

It is precisely this kind of invasion of "imperial proportions" and uncertain duration that now seems to be the main agenda of Washington's War on Terrorism. In the occupation and "nation-building" processes following invasions (as in the case of Afghanistan), explicit colonialism, in the most brazen nineteenth century sense, will be avoided. No formal annexation will take place, and at least a pretense of local rule will be established from the beginning, even during direct military occupation. Nevertheless, a central goal is to achieve some of what colonialism in its classic form previously accomplished. As Magdoff points out in this book,

> Colonialism, considered as the direct application of military and political force, was essential to reshape the social and economic institutions of many of the dependent countries to the needs of the metropolitan centers. Once this reshaping had been accomplished economic forces—the international price, marketing and financial systems—were by themselves sufficient to perpetuate and indeed intensify the relationship of dominance and exploitation between mother country and colony. In these circumstances, the colony could be granted formal political independence without changing anything essential, and without interfering too seriously with the interests which had originally led to the conquest of the colony.

Something of this sort is occurring in Afghanistan and is now being envisioned for Iraq should that country be invaded by the United States. Once a country has been completely disarmed and *reshaped* to fit the needs of the countries at the center of the capitalist world, "nation-building" will be complete and the occupation will presumably come to an end. But in areas that contain vital resources like oil (or that are deemed of strategic significance in gaining access to such resources), a shift back from formal to informal imperialism after an invasion may be slow to take place—or will occur only in very limited ways. "Informal control" or the mechanism of global accumulation that systematically favors the core nations, constitutes the normal means through which imperialist exploitation of the periphery operates. But this requires on occasion extraordinary means in order to bring recalcitrant states back into conformity with the market and with the international hierarchy of power with the United States at its apex.

At present U.S. imperialism appears particularly blatant because linked directly with war in this way, and pointing to an endless series of wars in the future to achieve essentially the same ends. However, if we wish to understand the underlying forces at work we should not let this heightened militarism and aggression distract us from the inner logic of imperialism, most evident in the rising gap in income and wealth between rich and poor countries, and in the net transfers of economic surplus from periphery to center that make this possible. The growing polarization of wealth and poverty between nations (a polarization that exists within nations as well) is the system's crowning achievement on the world stage. It is also what is ultimately at issue in the struggle against modern imperialism. As Magdoff argues in *Imperialism Without Colonies*, there is an essential oneness to economic, political and military domination under capitalism. Those seeking to oppose the manifestations of imperialism must recognize that it is impossible to challenge any one of these effectively without calling into question all the others—and hence the entire system.

Harry Magdoff's writings on imperialism from the 1960s and '70s, some of the most important of which are reproduced here, constitute an unparalleled guide to the historical dynamic of modern imperialism. They thus represent an invaluable resource to those engaged in the struggle of humanity to free itself from global exploitation—and from the seemingly endless wars of terror and destruction through which such exploitation is made possible.

NOTES

1   Richard N. Haass, "Imperial America," paper delivered at the Atlanta Conference, November 11, 2000 www.brook.edu.
2   Robert D. Kaplan, *Warrior Politics* (New York: Random House, 2002), pp. 147-49.
3   Michael Ignatieff, "The Burden," *New York Times Magazine*, January 5 2003, p. 24.
4   Prabhat Patnaik, "Whatever Happened to Imperialism?," *Monthly Review*, vol. 42, no. 6 (November 1990), pp. 1-6.
5   John Gallagher and Ronald Robinson, "The Imperialism of Free Trade," *The Economic History Review*, second series, vol. 6, no. 1 (1953), pp. 1-15. Gallagher and

Robinson were far from the first to apply the concepts of free trade imperialism and informal control to the study of the British Empire—although they provided perhaps the most cogent argument in this respect. See, for example, H.J. Habakkuk, "Free Trade and Commercial Expansion, 1853-1870," in J. Holland Rose, A.P. Newton and E.A. Benians, ed., *The Cambridge History of the British Empire* (Cambridge: Cambridge University Press, 1940), vol. 2, pp. 751-805. Similar arguments were presented by William Appleman Williams in his classic study *The Tragedy of American Diplomacy* (New York: W.W. Norton, 1959, 1962) and other works.

6   William W. Kauffman, *British Policy and the Independence of Latin America, 1804-1828* (New Haven: Yale University Press, 1951), p. 178.

7   Wolfgang J. Mommsen, *Theories of Imperialism* (Chicago: University of Chicago Press, 1980), pp. 86-87.

8   V.I. Lenin, *Imperialism, the Highest Stage of Capitalism* (New York: International Publishers, 1939), p. 85. A similar defense might be advanced for the non-Marxist Hobson. Although he saw imperialism as related to protectionism rather than free trade, and in that sense more closely related to colonialism, his analysis of imperialism was too rich and his understanding of its "economic taproot" too complex to reduce it to mere formal control. Thus he saw British imperialism in China as arising principally from commercial ends and facilitated at times by unequal treaties and even an "open door" policy. See J.A. Hobson, *Imperialism: A Study* (Ann Arbor: University of Michigan Press, 1938), p. 307.

9   Pierre Jalée, *The Pillage of the Third World* (New York: Monthly Review Press).

10   Henry Kissinger, *Does America Need a Foreign Policy?* (New York: Simon Schuster, 2001), p. 17.

11   "It's Not 'All About Oil' But…," *Business Week Online*, www.businessweek.com, January 30, 2003.

12   Richard N. Haass, *Intervention: The Use of American Military Force in the Post-Cold War World* (Washington D.C.: Brookings Institution Press, 1999), pp. 84, 134-35.

I. The Achievement of Paul Baran

PAUL BARAN was a social scientist and a Marxist. While economics was his major field of study, his interest in economics and his approach to the study of economic developments were part and parcel of his continuous search for a better understanding of human society: to find out how it operates and how it can be changed for the benefit of man. He found in Marx's studies and thought the most satisfactory explanation of how and why societies change, of the origin and development of capitalist society, and of the transformation of capitalist to socialist society. Baran surely knew as much about Marx's writings as any "Marx specialist." But he did not use this knowledge to become a mere commentator on or interpreter of Marx. Nor did he in his studies of contemporary society seek to fit the facts into a preconceived Marxist mold. Instead he adopted Marx's way of thinking: he virtually breathed Marxism. Not only did he absorb Marx's analyses, but he learned from Marx how to ask the important questions and how to seek out the significant relationships among the infinitude of economic and social phenomena. Confronted with changes in monopoly capitalism, in imperialism, and in the construction of socialism, he did not hunt up and rely on the appropriate quotation. Instead, he asked: how would a Marx tackle this problem? This meant persistent grappling and struggle with new facts and new theories to discover the significant and the relevant. It also meant a continuous re-examination of Marx's hypotheses in the light of new facts and developments.

Baran brought to his studies not only brilliance and a restless curiosity, but a well- trained and well-equipped mind. The fortunes of life led him to explore and learn from three different cultures—Russian, German, and Anglo-American. In Baran, these cultures blended well, and they enriched his knowledge and analytical competence.

Above all, Baran was a man of passion—passionate in the search for truth and about the uses to which this truth could be put. It was not truth in and of itself he wanted, but knowledge and understanding that would help eliminate poverty and other social ills. His credo was forcefully stated in "The Commitment of the Intellectual" (*Monthly Review*, May 1961). In his own words:

> The desire to tell the truth is therefore only one condition for being an intellectual. The other is courage, readiness to carry on rational inquiry to wherever it may lead, to undertake ruthless criticism of everything that exists, ruthless in the sense that the criticism will not shrink either from its own conclusions or from conflict with the powers that be (Marx). An intellectual is thus in essence a social critic, a person whose concern is to identify, to analyze, and in this way to help overcome the obstacles barring the way to the attainment of a better, more humane, and more rational social order.

The article from which this quotation is taken is itself illustrative of Baran's commitment. For this was not an article requested by the *Monthly Review* editors, and obviously, it was not one designed to enhance his professional prestige. He felt he had to write this article just as he had to cry out against the invasion of Cuba and against all the evils of imperialism: it was his responsibility as a student and a citizen. He was deeply troubled by the apathy and indifference of his fellow social scientists, and he wholeheartedly accepted the dictum of Goethe that "one must from time to time repeat what one believes in, proclaim what one agrees with and what one condemns."[1] Therefore, he had to speak his mind. Accepting Marx's thesis, "The Philosophers have only *interpreted* the world in various ways; the point, however, is to *change* it," he, in effect, insisted that by neglecting the need to change the world, social scientists in the United States have become false and impotent interpreters.

Passion and objectivity, by currently accepted standards, are considered to be mutually exclusive in the social sciences. It is conceded that a good general should and can, at one and the same time, be a man of passion and a cool-headed realist. But not the social scientist: he apparently cannot be trusted to recognize and respect the truth if he feels too strongly about it. Obviously, passion *can* interfere with objectivity, but it is equally true that the mere appearance of objectivity can serve to becloud the truth. Excessive interest in appearing to be objective can lead to ignoring the implicit assumptions about the permanence of the institutions studied and consequently to an unquestioning acceptance of the myths that have grown up in the process of attempting to guarantee this permanence. It can also lead to the restriction of studies to safe, if relatively insignificant, areas—those about which controversy can be conducted in gentlemanly fashion. A man like Baran could not accept passion and truth as mutually exclusive. Real objectivity, to him, meant facing up to the conflict between passion and the comprehension of reality. He understood that the influence of one upon the other and the struggle between the two were part of the process of the endless search for objective truth. Struggle was not alien to him. He saw himself as a fighter in all his activities: a fighter for knowledge, for the defeat of irrationality, for the progress of man.

The Quality of Baran's Thought

THE PATHS TO KNOWLEDGE and discovery are diverse. Explorers choose their routes in different ways, influenced by teachers, environment, and their own personalities. If one wishes to understand and appreciate an original thinker, it is not sufficient merely to classify him as, say, a Marxist. More important is what he selects from Marx for his own use and how he uses these aspects of Marx's thought.

While Baran appreciated the formal procedures of the typical academic study of economics and even enjoyed the aesthetics of mathematical reasoning, he did not pursue these lines of inquiry because in the main they do not lead to further understanding of the important issues of capitalist society and are too often a way to avoid the issues. Perfecting even such important tools of modern analysis as input-output and linear programming could contribute to greater efficiency of a planned economy, but would have little importance in transforming an irrational society into a rational one. To summarize his own program of studies, Baran chose this apt quotation from J. D. Bernal as the epigraph of his magnum opus, *The Political Economy of Growth*: "What social science needs is less elaborate techniques and more courage to tackle, rather than dodge, the central issues. But to demand that is to ignore the social reasons that have made social science what it is."

Baran's way toward better understanding of the central issues was to search for synthesis, for a unifying approach to the diverse trends in economics, politics, social problems, and culture. This is not to say that he expected to find a simple, all-embracing formula that would explain all of the different social and cultural phenomena. That would border on mysticism. The never-ending approach to synthesis meant for Baran that each phase of society was to be studied not as an isolate but in terms of how it is influenced by and in turn influences the rest of society. This does not mean providing a long list of all the possible interconnections, causal or temporal. It does mean trying to find those significant interrelationships which explain how the phenomena arise and disappear, and how they behave (or operate) in the environment in which they appear. From such study of the concrete in its own environment comes the ability to find the common elements, and therefore the generalizations, which lead to useful syntheses. But the process does not end there. For the syntheses must then be used to re-examine the concrete interrelations, both as a test of the generalizations and to anticipate new developments in society.

This approach is very different from the customary scholarly practices of our times. The separation of the disciplines, together with prevailing methods of education and training, inhibit even the more courageous thinkers. Since all the disciplines evolve according to their own rules, there is a tendency, greatly reinforced by bureaucratic impulses, for each in its isolation to become purer and more abstract. When the practitioners begin to feel uncomfortable because of the apparent sterility of their results, or when confronted with a too-obvious disparity between theory and reality, they begin to look elsewhere for new ideas. At such moments, the economists seek new insights from the sociologists, the sociologists from the political scientists, etc.; and usually a little amateur psychoanalysis is thrown in for good measure. But by this time it is too late. The old definitions and the habitual ways of thinking, arrived at in all their isolated purity, are encrusted. The addition of so-called new variables does not make for synthesis; it merely results in an eclectic jumble of ideas.

The strategic aspect of Baran's thought, following Marx's example, was to distinguish capitalist society from past and future societies and thus to study it as a developing organism. Instead of the mere addition of history and sociology to economics as in a cookbook recipe, examination of capitalism as a social system *sui generis* makes possible meaningful distinctions between attributes common to all societies and those unique to the capitalist system. This way of thinking provides the framework for examining concretely the interrelations of the different parts and enables the student to arrive at unifying principles to mark off different stages in capitalist society as it develops and changes.

This approach also implies a critical view. The analyst must search not only for the origins and effective causes of the growth of the system and its institutions, but also for the sources of its decline and transformation. To understand development and change one has persistently to look for the negative and understand the interaction and struggle between the negative and the positive, between the forces tending to preserve the status quo and the forces making for change. The role of critic suited Baran well. His contempt for complacency, his acute sense of irony, and his hatred of sham and irrationality added zest to his critical analysis of society. He was, however, a critic in the best sense of the term. Because the purpose of the criticism was a ruthless search for the truth, he looked for whatever could help in arriving at the truth. All new developments therefore had to be examined, all new ideas and theories had to be understood and evaluated. By the same token, prevailing myths and illusions parading under the banner of social science had to be exposed and fought. But this attack was to pave the way for a better understanding of reality. He was a critic of capitalist society, but, as with Marx, this was part of the movement toward a better society.

If Baran had a faith, it was his unshakable confidence in the ability of man to reason and to use his reason for human progress. Had he believed in Satan, his devil would have been irrationality. But objective reason, to Baran, was not God-given or independent of man: it was a product of man, anchored in man's expanding and deepening understanding of nature and society. Thus the pursuit of reason was the concrete exploration and practical exploitation of the natural and social conditions of progress. The irrationality to be fought was not only superstition and mysticism but the lack of faith in objective reason itself and in the ability of man to use it to improve his lot.

The Failures of Bourgeois Economics

THE BOURGEOIS ECONOMISTS' lack of faith in the objective reason of man was at the heart of Baran's quarrels with his colleagues. For the economists in their search for the rationale of a market economy come to believe that only through the market can an economy operate rationally. Just as in religion, to paraphrase Marx, the product of man's mind is personified in a God and set of rules that govern man's destiny, so does the anarchy of the market as conceived in the minds of economists become for them the true objective reason.[2] The faults economists find with economic affairs are attributed to interferences with the market by monopolies, by strong unions, by perverse governments. And those economists who are bold enough to question the all-embracing wisdom of the market, the agnostics, confine their remedies to political tinkering with the market.

The academic economists have not been able to accept Marx's critique of the fetishism of commodities or the conclusions that follow from it: the market is not the highest form of man's wisdom or a necessity of nature but a product and reflection of man-made social forces; the rationality of the market is that it is a rational medium for the operation of the institutions of capitalism, and it functions in such a fashion as to reproduce the social and economic relations of capitalism. Unable to recognize the nature of this connection between the market and social forces, bourgeois economists are equally unable to understand the limitations of their own analyses. The body of thought which appears to them to demonstrate the "rationality" of the market is in reality constructed of axioms and definitions which in effect assume the conclusions— sometimes explicitly, but more often implicitly by their treatment of economic phenomena in isolation and independent of their historic development.

As a result of these limitations, the academic economist is ill-equipped for objective study of the irrationality of the market economy as evidenced in such phenomena as persistent unemployment, poverty, super-exploitation of the Negro, waste, and stagnation. He is particularly at a loss when it comes to penetrating the relationship between the stagnation of the underdeveloped areas and the functioning of the advanced industrial nations. Especially alien to his way of thinking is the concept of the backward nations as an integral part of the market system of the advanced nations, the idea that the "rational" world markets and their institutions operate in such a fashion as to reproduce continuously the backwardness and economic dependency of the underdeveloped nations.

Bourgeois economic theory, in other words, is by its very nature incapable of explaining why capitalism induces rapid development of productive resources in a relatively small part of the world capitalist system and acts to restrict the growth of productivity in the rest of the capitalist world. Modern economic theory (after Ricardo and John Stuart Mill) grew and nourished by directing its attention to mechanical aspects of a market in equilibrium and how the market achieves equilibrium. The underlying questions asked by economists concerned the static aspects of an intrinsically harmonious system. The way of thought that evolved within the confining limits of static equilibrium study continue to dominate these economists' analyses when they alter their models and equations to try to explain dynamic changes over time. Even the Keynesian "revolution," although it incorporated a theoretical analysis of business fluctuations within the main body of economic thought, did not break through the limitations imposed by concentrating on the short run and avoiding the issues of secular growth and decline.

In recent years—starting just before the war, but especially in the postwar period—more and more economists have begun to explore the question of economic development. New tools had to be developed for this study, and interestingly enough they turned out to be either independent rediscoveries of Marx's tools or directly derived from Marx. But what is important about tools is how they are used, and it must unfortunately be said that these excursions into dynamic analysis, despite their formal affinity to Marxian thought, are usually quite sterile. The reason is that this dynamic analysis, although more and more mathematically refined, has all the weaknesses of the abstract, unhistorical method of traditional economic theory. Modern growth theory does not critically examine the fundamental assumptions of traditional economics to find out where it has gone wrong; the new theory is for the most part merely an appendage of the old.

The absence of a vital theory shows up clearly in the numerous studies of retardation of growth in underdeveloped countries. These studies are often excellent contributions to a descriptive examination of the various problems facing these societies. But their competence is usually restricted to the recital and documentation of a long bill of particulars of ills and evils. Attempts at diagnosis usually lead to concentration on one or two symptoms of the disease. Population is growing too rapidly, or the amount of capital is insufficient, or there are too few daring entrepreneurs. The proposed remedies, flowing from a superficial diagnosis, are necessarily concerned with symptoms rather than causes. It is not surprising that the frustrations produced by the contrast between theory and reality open the road to non-economic explanations. Dragged in, for example, are anthropological concepts of the incompatibility of value systems of different cultures, or psychological "explanations" of when and where dynamic elites (a fancy term for Western-style capitalists) have attained high social status.

Finally, the poverty of traditional economics, especially when it deals with development, results from the main taboos of the profession: against the use of socialist economic planning to develop productive resources and against analysis of the role of imperialism as an instrument in maintaining the backwardness of underdeveloped countries. In these respects, the situation today is, with the rarest of exceptions, as described by Veblen in *The Higher Learning in America* where he pointed out that the social scientists "are free to give the fullest expression to any conclusions or convictions to which their inquiries may carry them. That they are able to do so is a fortunate circumstance, due to the fact that their intellectual horizon is bounded by the same limits of commonplace insight and preconceptions as are the prevailing opinions of the conservative middle class."

These preconceptions are reflected in the worship of the rationality of the marketplace and the related inability to comprehend social revolutions which, through changing the class in control of economic and social power, take over the direction of the economy to achieve clearly defined goals. After all, how does one know whether such goals are rational if there is no free market by which to judge them? The economists are disturbed by the disruption of customary markets and the inevitable inefficiencies accompanying a revolution such as Cuba's, but they do not weigh these negative aspects against the fact that for the first time *all* Cuban children get first priority on a minimum amount of milk, or that at long last illiteracy is overcome. They hail the successes signalized by the rapid growth rate of the Mexican economy but do not recognize that this growth involves an allocation of economic resources such that 24 percent of the population over one year of age *never* eat meat, fish, milk, or eggs.[3]

This is not to say that academics as individuals do not sympathize with suffering, or are not aware of it. But their task, as "scientists," is to explain the existing social system and help to make it work better. Socialist economic planning is simply not on the agenda as an alternative to the reforms they propose. And here, as the case of imperialism vividly shows, national interest raises its head. An excellent illustration of the taboo against analyzing imperialism is the experience Paul Baran had in placing his path- breaking article, "On the Political Economy of Backwardness." It took some two years and numerous rejection letters before a publisher could be found for this forceful and brilliant statement of the thesis later expanded in *The Political Economy of Growth*. Two of the rejection letters belong side by side in a textbook on imperialism. One is from a world-famous British economist who explains most politely that despite the many virtues of the article, he could not very well accept it for publication since the model Baran draws of an underdeveloped country is much too general. Surely, Baran's description of the way imperialism works does not properly apply to present and former British colonies. Perhaps Baran's article would be closer to the truth if he restricted his model to Latin America. The rejection letter from a United States economist complained that while the study might be a useful review of backwardness and imperialism in the rest of the world, it surely didn't apply to Latin America, where progressive reforms were under way.

The article finally found a home in the relatively obscure *Manchester School of Economics and Social Studies*, January 1952. It caused a notable stir in the colonial world, including Latin America and the British sphere, where the

generalized descriptions of the nature and causes of backwardness were imme-
diately recognized and identified.

The reception given to this article was merely a foretoken of the excitement
aroused in underdeveloped countries by Baran's *Political Economy of Growth*.
Here, finally, was a full-dress analysis which could clear the way for developing
specific programs to transform stagnant and backward economies. No one real-
ized more clearly than Baran himself that his work was not the final word and
that much more study and research was needed. But his forthright analysis provides the framework and inspiration for further work along the avenues he
opened up. It also serves as a textbook to educate those who are going to do the
transforming, and as a useful guide to the tasks which must be undertaken.
Copies of this book on the shelves of the leaders of the Cuban Revolution are
well thumbed and heavily underlined. Just as it is an unusual sight to see a copy
of the book in United States bookshops, it is a rare bookstore in Mexico City,
for example, which does not prominently display a copy of the Spanish edition.

The Marxist Contribution

THE VITALITY AND SIGNIFICANCE of *The Political Economy of Growth*
stems from the fact that it is rooted in the Marxist way of thought. For the Marxist body of economic and social analysis provides the most effective apparatus
for understanding the problems of economic development. Marx's thought is
directed to precisely the problems of growth, class conflict, social change, and
transformation of societies; and these are the immediate problems of the underdeveloped world. Moreover, the method of analysis he used in studying society
as a developing organism and the differences produced by historic change provides the economist with tools specially designed to penetrate the complexity of
the underdeveloped societies, to lay bare, in Baran's term, the "morphology of
backwardness." (It is difficult to refrain from pointing out, in passing, the paradox that it is Marx, the critic, who provides the more effective instruments for
studying growth, because he paid so much attention to capital accumulation—
in terms of its historical origin and as the driving force of capitalism. The scientists of the status quo on the other hand, offer little help and frequently mis-
lead because their mental energies have been focused on equilibrium or, at best,
the mechanics of the business cycle.)

While Marx's work provided the key, some of the concepts and ways of
thought that later grew up in the Marxist environment had first to be cleared away.

One of the main obstacles to constructive analysis in this area was the acceptance, implicit or explicit, of a rigid framework of economic stages of social development. Since Western Europe went through a stage of feudalism before the stage of capitalism, and the stage of capitalism was to be the precursor of socialism, it was assumed by many followers of Marx that this progression was a necessary law of social development. It may be belaboring the obvious to emphasize here that such a concept is alien to scientific and, by the same token, to Marx's thinking. The hallmark of Marx's approach is the discovery of general truths about the specific changes that took place in the geographic areas and time periods he investigated, based on the evidence which was then available. From this, Marx distilled what he discovered to be the *necessary* interrelations—distinguishing between the primary and secondary elements—which explained the historical transformations of human societies. Acceptance of these generalizations as the most fruitful guide to explorations into questions of history and social science does not mean acceptance of a supra-historical design for all peoples, regardless of specific historical developments. Such acceptance would be mysticism, not science.

The search for a rigid, evolutionary, and "Marxist" pattern of social change induced an overemphasis on the feudal—or seemingly feudal—features of underdeveloped, colonial societies. The special stress on feudalism was based not so much on a critical examination of that form of society and the specific aspects of land relations but, quite frequently, on the preconceptions of the investigator and the superficial similarities between features of the country investigated and those of classic feudalism (usually an idealized representation of what feudalism was supposed to have been).[4] There was then superimposed upon this rigid pattern of development the role of imperialism in entrenching these seemingly feudal features. From this it was deduced that the middle classes were being prevented from breaking out of the feudal fetters because of the protection afforded the latter by political and economic imperialism. Hence there was bound to be a temporary identity of interests in the struggle for national independence between the oppressed masses and those members of the bourgeoisie who are nationalistic in spirit and, in addition, want to eliminate the protectors of the feudalistic restrictions on the growth of industrial capitalism. The time elapsing between the transition from feudalism to capitalism and the transition from capitalism to socialism might be relatively short, but a two-stage evolution along these lines was the most reasonable pattern to expect.

Implied in this viewpoint are several assumptions: 1) Important sections of the bourgeoisie will not only support the fight for political independence but

will also support the measures needed for economic independence from imperialism. 2) Economic independence can be achieved without disrupting (or
destroying) the trade channels, financial institutions, and market relations
(including the price-and-profit structure) on which the "independence-striving" bourgeoisie depend for their prosperity. 3) After imperialist domination
and feudal fetters are removed, the national bourgeoisie can achieve fairly
rapid industrialization, under today's conditions, without the assistance of
state-protected monopolies which would act as fetters on the competition
needed for the spread of industrialization. And 4) the fetters of feudalism-
imperialism can either be removed without the revolutionary participation of
the oppressed classes; or if these classes do participate, they will carry out the
revolution without insisting on additional goals inimical to the interests of the
industrializing bourgeoisie.

The above characterization of the "rigid" Marxist analysis and its implications has been deliberately exaggerated in an attempt to clarify the value of
Baran's contribution. In fact, Baran, in my opinion, was influenced by some of
these preconceptions and did not make a complete breakthrough. But his independence of thought, intensive study, and talent for synthesis enabled him to
present an extremely valuable extension of the analysis of imperialism, one
which is a closer approach to reality, and, as indicated above, points the way to
more realistic study and the development of more effective programs.

Baran's Analysis of Underdevelopment

THE PRESENT EXAMINATION of Baran's contribution to economic and
social thought is focused on his analysis of underdevelopment. He has given us
light and wisdom in other fields as well. The bulk of his work in other fields,
including the part in his *Political Economy of Growth* not discussed here, is concerned with the analysis of monopoly capitalism in the United States. His work
on this subject will no doubt appear in a more finished form in the forthcoming
volume written in collaboration with Paul M. Sweezy than in earlier, piecemeal
essays and chapters. It is only proper that an evaluation of this part of his work
should wait until the eagerly expected volume by the two Pauls is published.[5]

Mention must be made, however, of the concept of the economic surplus
which Baran used as a unifying analytical device in studying monopoly capitalism in advanced industrialist societies, problems of underdevelopment, and the
construction of a socialist society. While the inspiration for the concept as used

by Baran stems from Marx, it is important to recognize that there is a very important difference between Baran's use of the "economic surplus" concept and Marx's theory of surplus value.

Marx sought in his theory of value and surplus value—taking into account the historical and analytical development (the inner logic à la Hegel) of these concepts—a unifying set of principles with which to explain the origins of capitalism and the nature of its growth, development, and decline. The theory was designed to explain, among other things, 1) the historical development of capital itself and its change from merchant to industrial capital; 2) the distribution of income and the struggles over the distribution of income; 3) the nature and limits of the economic and political struggle over the length of the working day and conditions of work in the factory; 4) the rise of productivity and the advance of technology; and 5) the drive to accumulate capital, from its historical origin in primary accumulation to its position as the controlling force in the expansion and contraction of capitalist economies. The accomplishment of all this required a complex analytical construction and a technical consistency. For Marx not only attempted to show how the exchange process continuously re-creates, via value- exchange and surplus value, the social compulsions of capitalist relations; he also attempted to explain how the capitalist economy, working through the market, reproduces itself and at the same time creates the conditions for the expansion of internal markets and the accumulation of capital.

Now the complex, technical concept of surplus value has at its foundation a much simpler idea: an economy, with a given technique of production, can continue operating at a given level only if it can provide enough goods to keep the workers alive and working and to replace the tools used in production; an economy can grow only if it can produce an excess—a surplus—over the amount needed to replace the worker and his tools. The surplus—its size and its method of use—determines the growth potential of an economy. Marx's theory was hammered out to explain how this surplus is created and used in the historical development and operation of capitalism. Baran, on the other hand, used only the "simple" concept of the economic surplus (enriched by Marx's study and theory), and he used it as a more general device, to some extent for pedagogic purposes. For Baran does not examine the actual surplus in all its phases of development; in this respect, he took Marx's work for granted and focused his own attention primarily on what he called the *potential* surplus. The latter is an active, operative concept: it leads to an understanding of the waste, inefficiency, and unfulfilled possibilities of monopoly capitalism; it also leads to the recognition that the real needs of underdeveloped societies for substantial progress can be met only by a new social and economic organization that can mobilize the potential surplus and put it to use in the interests of the people.

Baran's diagnosis is rich in detail and encompasses subtle variations in the problems of different parts of the globe. We must content ourselves with a bare outline of his argument.

Baran argues that the root causes of the economic and social backwardness in our age are to be found in imperialism. Imperialism operated differently in India, Africa, Latin America, and other colonial areas, conditioned by variations in historical circumstances in the mother country and in the colonial areas themselves. But the forces of imperialism, whatever specific forms they may take, have had a similar effect in the dominated countries: to harden and strengthen the sway of *merchant* capitalism in the colonial nations and to slow down, if not entirely prevent, the transformation of this merchant capitalism into *industrial* capitalism.

Imperialist power achieved a stable and servile society by, on the one hand, protecting and strengthening a feudal-mercantile order, and on the other hand, preventing the development of a revolutionary middle-class by economically strangling indigenous industrial capitalism. The resulting social systems in these areas are under the control of a political and social coalition of wealthy compradors, monopolists granted special favor by the state, and large landowners—all dedicated to the defense of the existing economic structure and its established ties to the metropolitan center.

The net effect of this type of social and economic structure is a slow and lopsided growth, partly stimulated by investments and technical know-how from the Western world and by charity. The slow growth is usually dissipated by rapid population growth, corruption in government, and the squandering of resources by the ruling oligarchy. The causes of the slow growth are definitely *not* those identified by the academic economists: shortage of capital, lack of entrepreneurial talent, or overpopulation. These are symptoms, not causes, and they reflect the existing social and economic organization.

A substantive change from slow growth—and the hunger, disease, and misery associated with it—can only be accomplished by major and far-reaching structural changes. Large investments in construction and machinery, long-term planning, and overcoming tradition-bound patterns of work and thought are needed for such nations to shift into high gear and achieve a large and continuous enough increase in output and productive capacity to outstrip population growth and bring about a meaningful rise in living conditions.

But this means a sweeping reorganization of society, an all-out mobilization of creative potentials, and appropriating and controlling the economic surplus now flowing into the pockets of the wealthy.

A necessary condition for effecting such a sweeping reorganization of society is political national independence—freedom from the direct control of a foreign state or the indirect, more "democratic," control of a strong imperialist power. Given political independence, according to Baran, some of the obstacles to economic and social development can be overcome. But it does not eliminate either the oppression and exploitation of the peasantry by the landed aristocracy or the strangulation of industrial development by monopoly business.

Furthermore, imperialism as an effective system of control is not automatically removed by political independence. The economic structure that was built as part of the market system and the investment pattern of the metropolitan center lives on. And with it *economic* dependence lives on. Meanwhile, the tenuous coalitions of socially heterogeneous groups that rule the newly independent nations are faced with processes of disintegration, speeded up by an intensification of internal class conflict resulting from rising popular aspirations to social as well as national liberation.

The only rational solution of the problems of backwardness and economic dependence is socialist economic planning. Requiring a change in the location of class power, a removal of control over economic resources from the partners of imperialist powers, it offers the medium for mobilizing an economic surplus far in excess of the "normal" surplus and an opportunity for effective utilization of the surplus for rapid growth of productive powers.

Significant economic developments, whether under socialist economic planning or as a breakthrough in a capitalist framework, are inimical to the interests of the dominant classes in the advanced capitalist nations. The task of imperialism in our time is therefore to slow down and *control* economic development. In place of the white man's burden and the introduction of "civilization," economic development guided by the metropolis becomes the rationalization of today's imperialism. The claws behind this liberalism appear when a country takes off under its own steam toward economic development, sometimes only when the first baby-steps are taken.

Since Baran's book was published, his thesis on the opposition of imperialism to independent economic development has been all too well substantiated in one way or another by actions of the United States and other imperialist powers in Guatemala, Cuba, British Guiana, Brazil, Vietnam, Malaysia, and the Congo.

To get the full significance of Baran's contribution, the entire book has to be read and studied. There we can learn much from the spirit as well as from the substance, and we can hardly fail to be moved by its eloquent concluding paragraph:

> To contribute to the emergence of a society in which development will supplant stagnation, in which growth will take the place of decay, and in which culture will put an end to barbarism is the noblest, and, indeed, the only true function of intellectual endeavor. The need for the triumph of reason over myth, for the victory of life over death cannot be proved by means of logical inference. As a great physicist [Max Planck] once said, "Logic alone is incapable of carrying anyone beyond the realm of his own perception; it cannot even compel him to recognize the existence of his fellow men." This need must rest on the proposition that humanity's claim to life, to development, to happiness requires no justification. With this proposition it stands and falls. This proposition is, however, its sole unprovable and irrefutable premise.

2.   The New Imperialism

A FOCAL POINT OF LENIN'S THEORY of imperialism is the classification of imperialism as a special stage in the development of capitalism, arising toward the end of the 19th century. This attempt to give imperialism such a specific historical reference date has been a subject of controversy, the main objection being that many of the features considered characteristic of imperialism are found early in the game and throughout the history of capitalism: the urgency to develop a world market, the struggle to control foreign sources of raw materials, the competitive hunt for colonies, and the tendency toward concentration of capital.

Some scholars get around this problem by distinguishing between an "old" and a "new" imperialism. Whatever semantic device is used, there are good and sufficient reasons for clearly marking off a new period in the affairs of world capitalism. Of the many distinguishing features of this new stage, two, in my opinion, are decisive: First, England is no longer the undisputed leading industrial power. Strong industrialized rivals appear on the scene: the United States, Germany, France, and Japan. Second, within each of the industrialized nations, economic power shifts to a relatively small number of big integrated industrial and financial firms.

The framework for these developments was provided by the introduction during the last 20 to 30 years of the 19th century of new sources of energy and a new departure in technology, which Veblen called "the technology of physics and chemistry." This is a technology that is based on the direct application of science and scientific research, rather than on mere mechanical ingenuity. It was in the final 30 years of the 19th century that:

> . . . a whole century of slow progress and restatement in pure science—particularly in thermodynamics, electromagnetism, chemistry and geology—began to

meet up with rapid development in practical mechanical engineering—and particularly in the production of machine-tools—and in industrial methods . . . not
only were new industries developed and new sources of power provided—the
internal combustion engine, stemming from progress in thermodynamics theory, being only less important than electricity. Innumerable existing industries—
mining and road-building, steel, agriculture, petroleum, concrete are but a few
examples—were transformed and expanded. Innumerable new products—the
modern bicycle, the telephone, the typewriter, linoleum, the pneumatic tyre,
cheap paper, artificial silk, aluminum, ready- made clothing and shoes—were
manufactured and marketed for the first time. It was in this period that mechanization first became characteristic of industry in general....[1]

Even more important than the technological features of this period per se is that
this technology as a rule required investment of large amounts of capital and
large production units. The main developments that characterize the transformation occurred in steel, electricity, industrial chemistry, and oil.[2]

Steel. Steel has unique properties that are essential in the construction of
machines such as internal combustion engines, electric generators, and steam
turbines. It was the introduction of steel rails and locomotives that made possible the carrying of heavy loads at high speeds. This reduced the cost of transport and provided the means for transforming local and regional businesses into
large, national industries.

Before the application of scientific methods, steel was practically a semi-pre-
cious metal. "Until [Bessemer and open-hearth] processes were introduced
steel making was hardly more than an empirical craft operation...."[3] The Besse-
mer process, introduced in 1854, still had limitations for the use of iron ore
available in the United States and Europe. The open-hearth method introduced
in the 1860's, and finally the "basic process" developed by Thomas and
Gilchrist in 1875 made possible the control of the carbon content of steel within very close limits—and opened up the age of steel. Techniques for improving
the properties of steel by use of alloys—to obtain the qualities needed for tool
steel, armaments, and stainless steel—were developed between 1870 and 1913.
Note that during the period 1870–1874 an average of 1 million tons of steel were
produced worldwide; during 1900–1904, the annual average world production
had risen to over 27 million tons.[4]

Electricity. While scientific experiments with electricity and theoretical
exploration of the subject go back to the 18th century, the application of these

experiments and theory to form a large-scale industry occurs toward the end of the 19th century. The first commercial generating stations in London, Milan, and New York were opened in the 1880s. The importance of electricity is not limited to its use as a new source of light, heat, and power. It is necessary, for example, in the refinement of copper and aluminum and the bulk production of caustic soda. (The invention of the process for commercial production of aluminum also stems from this period, occurring in 1886.) For manufacturing processes in general, the application of electricity made possible the kind of precise control which permitted the more complete mechanization on which modern mass-production industry depends.

Industrial Chemistry. Chemical processes in metallurgy, tanning, and fermentation had been known and used for many centuries. But industrial chemistry as a separate and large-scale industry originates in the last third of the 19th century. Here again the transformation is due to theoretical and experimental discoveries in science. The ability to synthesize organic chemicals in industrial processes could not appear before the proper understanding of chemical transformations was achieved. Thus the ability to determine the correct number of atoms in a molecule became possible once there was general recognition around 1860 of the law that equal volumes of gases under the same conditions contain the same number of molecules. The effective concept of the structural arrangement of atoms in a molecule comes in 1865. In contrast with the former almost accidental advances in organic chemistry, the new scientific achievements created the basis for new mass-production industries. The Solvay ammonia soda process and the catalytic processes for the manufacture of sulphuric acid and of ammonia belong also to the same period.

Oil. Here we are not dealing so much with technical and scientific advances as with the discovery and exploration of underground petroleum sources, though of course technical and scientific achievements are significant both in the techniques of extracting crude oil and in petroleum refining. From the historical point of view, it should be noted that large quantities of oil were first discovered in Pennsylvania in 1859. The Standard Oil Company was founded in 1870. Diamond drilling, the effective technique for piercing hard formations, was first invented in 1864 and was introduced in the United States in the 1870's.

The earliest phase of large oil discoveries was concerned with nationwide and international distribution systems for oil in kerosene lamps and for the manufacture of lubricants. The introduction of oil as fuel in industry and transportation follows from later discoveries of oil sources.

Sometimes referred to as a "second industrial revolution," these new phenomena were integral to the shift from a capitalism characterized by dispersed
small competitive units to one in which large concentrations of economic power
dominated the industrial and financial scene. How significant these late 19th
century technological developments were in accelerating monopolistic trends
can be seen by examining the giant corporations of today:

- Of the 50 largest industrial corporations in the United States today, 26
  (accounting for 62 percent of the total assets of the whole group) are in steel,
  oil, electrical equipment, chemicals, and aluminum.
- Of the 50 largest industrial corporations in capitalist countries outside the
  United States, 30 (accounting for 73 percent of the total assets of the group)
  are in these same industries.

The Rise of Big Business

OUR ARGUMENT HERE is not that the new technology determined the size
of the corporation and the monopolistic trends that accompanied Big Business.
Rather, the new technology provided the framework, and often the opportunity, for the quite normal tendencies of capitalist industry toward concentration of
power. For example, the transcontinental railroad and its feeders created the
possibility for local manufacturers to compete on a national scale. The overex-
pansion of production that resulted from many local producers' expanding their
capacity to meet the enlarged markets resulted in ruthless competition, failures,
mergers, and alliances—a familiar pattern of business history. The transformation that took place in the United States business life during the onset of the
imperialist stage is well summarized by Professor Chandler:

> In the 1870s, the major industries serviced an agrarian economy. Except for a few
> companies equipping the rapidly expanding railroad network, the leading
> industrial firms processed agricultural products and provided farms with food
> and clothing. These firms tended to be small, and bought their raw materials and
> sold their finished goods locally. Where they manufactured for a market more
> than a few miles away from the factory, they bought and sold through commis-
> sioned agents who handled the business of several other similar firms.
>
> By the beginning of the twentieth century, many more companies were mak-
> ing producers' goods, to be used in industry, rather than on the farm or by the

ultimate consumer. Most of the major industries had become dominated by a few large enterprises. These great industrial corporations no longer purchased and sold through agents, but they had their own nation-wide buying and marketing organizations. Many, primarily those in die extractive industries, had come to control their own raw materials In other words, the business economy had become industrial. Major industries were dominated by a few firms that had become great, vertically integrated, centralized enterprises. (Emphasis added.)[5]

The Civil War and the railroad expansion provided the opportunity for the maturation of powerful financial institutions that could accumulate the capital and organize the mergers that became what Chandler identifies as the "great, vertically integrated, centralized enterprises."[6] The new technological innovations discussed above provided the material production bases for such Big Business. The frequent depressions that began in 1873 were the battleground. And the method of business organization for this transformation was the corporation— what Veblen termed the "master institution of civilized life."

The New Drive for Raw Materials

THE NEW INDUSTRIES, the new technology and the rise of competition among industrialized nations gave a new importance to the role of raw materials. The struggle for the control of iron ore and coking coal on the European continent is a familiar story. Even more important was the pressure to gain control over distant territories whose value assumed new relevance. Barraclough summarizes this trend as follows:

. . . . the voracious appetite of the new industrialism, unable of its very nature to draw sufficient sustenance from local resources, rapidly swallowed up the whole world. It was no longer a question of exchanging European manufactures—predominantly textiles—for traditional oriental and tropical products, or even of providing outlets for the expanding iron and steel industries by building railways, bridges and the like. *Industry now went out into the world in search of the basic materials without which, in its new forms, it could not exist.* (Emphasis added.)[7]

This was part of a general new pattern of economic relations in the world capitalist system. During the period from 1860 to 1900, three changes in the economic relations between nations arc notable: 1) the number of commodities entering international trade on a large scale multiplied greatly; 2) competition between many widely separated regions of the world first appeared or grew more intense; and 3) the standard of living of workers and the profitability of industry in European nations came to depend on maintenance of overseas supplies, while the standard of living of the producers of raw materials came to depend on market fluctuations occurring sometimes on the other side of the world.[8]

As the need for raw materials grew, the rate of discovery and exploitation of the resources increased. "It was the same thirty years [from 1870 to 1900] that most of the undeveloped agricultural areas of the world were opened up and that, with the increase of geological knowledge, though not all were yet exploited, most of the world's great mineral-bearing districts were discovered."[9] It was in the last quarter of the 19th century that nickel was discovered and developed in Canada, copper and zinc in Australia, nitrogen in Chile, and tin and rubber in Malaya. In sum:

> The ring of distant primary producers was widened from North America, Roumania and Russia to tropical and sub-tropical lands and, beyond them, to Australasia and South Africa. *Areas and lines of commerce that had previously been self-contained dissolved into a single economy on a world scale.* (Emphasis added.)[10]

Advance in Ocean Transportation and the World Market

WORLD COMMERCE, as noted earlier, was an essential ingredient of early capitalism and it progressed as capitalism matured. But a new leap forward, involving the feasibility of moving cheaply the bulk raw materials needed for the new giant industries, was made possible by the mass production of steel and technical innovations in shipbuilding. Metal-built steamships using steel hulls, steel boilers, twin screws, and compound engines—a "synthesis of existing inventions"—became the predominant form of ocean transport in the last two decades of the 19th century.[11] The problems posed by the higher pressures needed in marine engines "were not solved till the later 1870's and early 1880's when improved steel boilers and tubes enabled shipbuilders to construct ships with triple expansion engines that worked at 150 lb. pressure and more."[12]

The demand for efficient and cheap bulk shipment of heavy products throughout the world, the new metal steamship which made it possible, and rapid communication (trans-Atlantic cable service began in 1866) set the stage for a commercial revolution. This commercial revolution was financed by the simultaneous growth of international banking and the creation of a "single multilateral system of international payments. A world market, governed by world prices, emerged for the first time."[13]

Empire and the New Imperialism

THE ABOVE DEVELOPMENTS also contributed to a speed-up in the industrialization of lands other than England—the United States, Germany, Japan, France, Belgium, and others. This industrialization occurred under circumstances in which concentration of economic power in large business units, mobilization of large masses of capital for particular projects, growth of protective tariffs, and a wave of militarization[14] provided the framework for what was essentially new in the imperialism of the late 19th and 20th centuries. Above all, what was new was the extension of imperialist behavior patterns to most industrialized nations.[15] It was no longer Britain controlling international commerce, carving out spheres of commercial influence, and picking up a colony here and there. Instead, it was the economic and political operations of other rapidly advancing countries rushing for their place in the sun which pinned a new label on modern society.

Under the impetus of this new imperialism no corner of the earth was left untouched: the entire world was transformed and adapted to the needs of the new dominant industry in each industrialized nation, and to the rivalry between these nations under the pressure of these needs.

Imperialism and Colonies

THE COMPLEX of economic and political relations that arose from or were an accommodation to these specially new phenomena encompasses the imperialist era. The change thus marked off is not an abrupt one; it flows directly from well-entrenched tendencies inherent in a capitalist economy. The principal new feature is the concentration of economic power in giant corporations and financial institutions, with the consequent internationalization of capital.

The urge to dominate is integral to business. Risks abound in the business world. Internal and external competition, rapid technological changes, depressions, to name but a few, threaten not only the rate of profit but the capital investment itself. Business therefore is always on the lookout for ways of controlling its environment—to eliminate as much risk as possible. In industry after industry, the battle for survival has also been a battle for conquest, from which the giant corporations best fitted for their environment have emerged. Their ways and habits are the result of a process of adaptation to the battle for survival and growth; these ways and habits have been built into their organizational structures and their modes of operation as ways of guaranteeing and sustaining victory.

1) The most obvious first requirement to assure safety and control in a world of tough antagonists is to gain control over as much of the sources of raw materials as possible—*wherever these raw materials may be, including potential new sources.*[16]

Controlling raw materials sources is both a protective device against pressure of competitors as well as a weapon of offense to keep non-integrated competitors in line. Ownership of and control over raw material supplies is, as a rule, an essential prerequisite for the ability of a leading firm or group of leading firms to limit new competition and to control production and prices of the finished products. Moreover, the very size of the large vertically integrated firms gives them the resources to explore and develop potential new supplies throughout the world.[17] The history of the oil industry is of course a classic illustration, but this principle applies also to the aluminum, steel, copper, and other industries.

2) The pattern of most successful manufacturing businesses includes conquest of foreign markets. This is so even where there is as large an internal market as in the United States. In the mass market auto industry, for example, foreign markets exercised an important influence from the earliest days. The sixth Ford car built was shipped to a Canadian distributor. The Ford Motor Company in its first year of operation started making arrangements for building up its foreign markets.[18]

Despite the very high rate of domestic population increase and the opportunities available in the underdeveloped regions of this country, the drive to develop exports of manufactures took root during the very first flush of industrial maturity—less than a decade after the end of the Civil War. In 1871 little over 7 percent of United States exports consisted of finished manufactures; by 1890 this percent rose to almost 12 percent; by 1900 to almost 19 percent.[19] The succession of depressions from 1873 to the turn of the century produced two responses: internally, a wave of consolidations and the move toward Big Business; externally, the drive to capture export markets, including those of industrialized Europe.[20]

The dynamics of this search for export markets varies from industry to industry, and has different degrees of importance at various stages in the evolution of an industry and in different phases of the business cycle. What must be understood in any case is the special significance for industry to maintain these export markets. Lenin's generalization on this point is most appropriate: "The growth of internal exchange, and particularly of international exchange, is the characteristic distinguishing feature of capitalism. The uneven and spasmodic character of the development of individual enterprises, of individual branches of industry and individual countries, is inevitable under the capitalist system."[21]

Foreign markets are pursued (with the aid and support of the state) to provide the growth rate needed to sustain a large investment of capital and to exploit new market opportunities. In this process, the dependence on export markets becomes a permanent feature, for these markets coalesce with the structure of industrial capacity. In one period exports may be the only way out of disaster; in another they may be the best way to maintain the flow of profits. But as the filling of foreign orders becomes built into the capacity and overhead of the business firm, the pressure to maintain these foreign markets over the long run becomes ever more insistent—especially as competitors arrive on the scene.[22]

3) Foreign investment is an especially effective method for the development and protection of foreign markets. The clearest historic demonstration of this was the export of capital for railways, which stimulated at the same time the demand for rails, locomotives, railway cars, and other products of the iron, steel, and machine industries.[23]

But this method of penetrating foreign markets becomes ever more prevalent in the age of the giant corporation, characterized as it is by intensification of national rivalries. The role of foreign investment to capture and exploit sources of raw materials is evident. More than this, though, is the urgency of foreign investment to withstand the competition, or to pre-empt markets, in the countries where competitive corporate giants also exist.

The foreign corporate giants can swing their own weight in controlling their own domestic markets, or in their preferential markets—such as in colonies, dependencies, or "spheres of influence." They can also use their political strength to set up protective tariffs and other trade barriers against outsiders. For these reasons, the ability to compete in other countries and to exercise the kind of market control needed by the giant corporations calls for a program of foreign investment. The competition between corporate giants resolves itself either in cartel arrangements or in permanent invasion of each others' markets via the route of foreign investment. Moreover, this procedure becomes more feasible in the age of Big Business, thanks to the large masses of capital available to large corporations from their own profits or from what they can mobilize in cooperation with financial institutions.

The foregoing reasons for the spurt of foreign investment in the age of imperialism are far from exhaustive. There is naturally the attractiveness of increasing
profit rates by taking advantage of lower labor costs abroad. Observe, for example,
how the Chase Manhattan Bank slips in information on wage rates in South Korea
in its report spelling out the attractiveness of investing in that country.

> In fact, the main impetus for Korea's economic growth comes from the determi-
> nation and drive of its businessmen and officials. Americans comment on the
> dexterity and aptitude of Korean workers, who are available at cash wage rates
> averaging 65c a day in textiles and 88c a day in electronics. These human char-
> acteristics produce industrial results.[24]

Attractive as lower costs are, their appeal is not necessarily the main attraction of
foreign investment. It is merely one of the influences. Much more important is the
spur of developing raw material resources, creating demand for exports, and taking advantage of "monopoly" situations. The latter arises due to cost advantages
of Big Business, exclusive patents, superior technology, or preferred market
demand stimulated by establishment of desired brands via sales promotion. Finally, foreign investment arises from the pressure to establish trade in markets protected by tariff walls or trade preferences. (United States investment in Canada, for
example, is a convenient arrangement for participating in British Empire trade.)

The commonly held notion that the theory of imperialism should be concerned largely with investment in underdeveloped countries just isn't correct.
The fact is that profitable investment opportunities in such countries are limited by the very conditions imposed by the operations of imperialism. Restricted
market demand and industrial backwardness are products of the lopsided economic and social structures associated with the transformation of these countries into suppliers of raw materials and food for the metropolitan centers.

Our purpose here is not to analyze exhaustively all the factors involved in
foreign investment. Rather, it is to suggest that there are clear reasons for the
spur of foreign investment in the age of imperialism—as a consequence of the
opportunities and pressures accompanying the rise of Big Business. This is not
prompted by the malice of the businessman, but by the normal and proper functioning of business in the conditions confronted. The patterns of these investments should be examined in their historical context, in light of the actual situations business firms deal with, rather than in the more usual terms of an
abstraction concerning the pressure of surplus capital.[25]

4) The drive for foreign investment opportunities and control over foreign markets brings the level of political activity on economic matters to a new and intense level. The last quarter of the 19th century sees the spread of protective tariffs.[26] Other political means—threats, wars, colonial occupation—are valuable assistants in clearing the way to exercise sufficient political influence in a foreign country to obtain privileged trade positions, to get ownership of mineral rights, to remove obstacles to foreign trade and investment, to open the doors to foreign banks and other financial institutions which facilitate economic entry and occupation.

The degree and type of political operation naturally vary. In weak outlying territories, colonial occupation is convenient. In somewhat different circumstances, bribery of officials or loans (via banks or state institutions) are appropriate.[27] Among the more advanced countries, alliances and interest groups are formed.

The result of these developments is a new network of international economic and political relations. The network itself changes in shape and emphasis over time as a result of wars, depressions, and differential rates of industrialization.[28] The forms also vary: colonies, semi- colonies, "a variety of forms of dependent countries—countries, which, officially, are politically independent, but which are in fact, enmeshed in the net of financial and diplomatic dependence,"[29] and junior and senior partners among the imperialist powers. The significant theme is the different degrees of dependence in an international economy, an international economy in continuous ferment as a result of the battles among giant corporations over the world scene and the operations of these corporations along with their state governments to maintain domination and control over weaker nations.

The oversimplification which identifies imperialism with colonialism pure and simple neither resembles Lenin's theory nor the facts of the case. Similarly fallacious is the version of Lenin's theory that imperialism is in essence the need of advanced countries to get rid of a surplus which chokes them, and that this surplus is divested through productive investments in colonies.

The stage of imperialism, as we have tried to show, is much more complex than can be explained by any simple formula. The drive for colonies is not only economic but involves as well political and military considerations in a world of competing imperialist powers. Likewise, the pressures behind foreign investment are more numerous and more involved than merely exporting capital to backward countries. There is no simple explanation for all the variations of real economic and political changes, nor is it fruitful to seek one. The special value of Lenin's theory is the highlighting of all the principal levers that have moved international economic relations. These levers are the ones associated with the new stage of monopoly and the essential ways monopoly operates to achieve, wherever and whenever feasible, domination and control over sources of supply and over markets. The fact that these are still the principal levers explains why the theory is still relevant. But the particular forms in which these factors operate and become adapted to new conditions requires continuous re-examination.

Modern Features of Imperialism

THE IMPERIALISM OF TODAY has several distinctly new features. These are, in our opinion: 1) the shift of the main emphasis from rivalry in carving up the world to the struggle against the contraction of the imperialist system; 2) the new role of the United States as organizer and leader of the world imperialist system; and 3) the rise of a technology which is international in character.

1) The Russian Revolution marks the beginning of the new phase. Before the Second World War the main features were the expansion of imperialism to cover the globe, and the conflicts among the powers for the redistribution of territory and spheres of influence. After the Russian Revolution, a new element was introduced into the competitive struggle: the urge to reconquer that part of the world which had opted out of the imperialist system and the need to prevent others from leaving the imperialist network. With the end of the Second World War, the expansion of the socialist part of the world and the break-up of most of the colonial system intensified the urgency of saving as much as possible of the imperialist network and reconquering the lost territories. Conquest in this context takes on different forms, depending on the circumstances: military and political as well as economic.

While the imperialist powers did not give up the colonies gladly or easily, the main purposes of colonialism had been achieved prior to the new political independence: the colonies had been intertwined with the world capitalist markets; their resources, economies, and societies had become adapted to the needs of the metropolitan centers. The current task of imperialism now became to hold on to as many of the economic and financial benefits of these former colonies as possible. And this of course meant continuation of the economic and financial dependency of these countries on the metropolitan centers.

Neither in the period right after the Russian Revolution nor in our own day does the central objective of extending and/or defending the frontiers of imperialism signify the elimination of rivalries among the imperialist powers. However, since the end of the Second World War this central objective has dominated the scene because of the increasing threat to the imperialist system and because of the greater unity among the powers imposed by United States leadership.[30]

2) Up to the end of the Second World War political and military operations in the imperialist world system were carried on in the traditional method of alignment in blocs: competitive interests in one bloc were temporarily repressed for the sake of a joint offense or defense against another bloc. The composition of these blocs changed over time as did the tactical advantages sought. Since 1945 the new phenomenon is the assumption by the United States of leadership of the entire imperialist system. As a result of its maturing economic and military strength and the destruction inflicted on rivals by the war, the United States had the capacity and the opportunity to organize and lead the imperialist network of our time.

The organizing of the postwar imperialist system proceeded through the medium of the international agencies established toward the end of the war: the United Nations, the World Bank, and the International Monetary Fund—in each of which the United States was able, for various reasons, to exercise the leading role. The system was consolidated through the activities of UNRRA, the Marshall Plan, and the several economic and military aid programs financed and controlled from Washington.

The new perspective of United States leadership was referred to indirectly by Secretary of State Rusk when he called attention to the fact that the United States is "criticized not for sacrificing our national interests to international interests but for endeavoring to *impose the international interest upon other nations.*" (Emphasis added.) This criticism is not rejected by the Secretary of State. Indeed, he is proud of it: "This criticism is, I think, a sign of strength—of our strength and the strength of international law." Further, he continues to spell out the ambitious vista of United States foreign policy:

But we know we can no longer find security and well-being in defenses and policies which are confined to North America, or the Western Hemisphere, or the North Atlantic community.

This has become a very small planet. We have to be concerned with all of it—with all of its land, waters, atmosphere, and with surrounding space.[31]

In view of the limitations of the United Nations, stemming from participation of socialist countries, the practical administration of this global and spatial concern was affected by a series of treaties and declarations covering the non-socialist world.

These diplomatic arrangements were stimulated and given substance by the proliferation of military bases around the planet. The new role of the United States in this respect can be seen in the fact that U.S. armed forces in the 1920's were stationed in only three countries abroad. During the Second World War, U.S. armed forces were to be found in 39 countries. Today, through distribution of military assistance and the direction of military training of foreign armies, U.S. military groups are located in at least 64 countries. These, as can be seen in Table I, are well spread out over the globe. That these forces and their equipment have not remained idle and that their presence exerts influence, even in the absence of direct action, is too obvious to need spelling out.

TABLE 1   *Number of Countries in which US. Armed Forces are Represented*

LATIN AMERICA	19	*Source*: From date in Agency
EAST ASIA (Including Australia)	10	for International Develop-
AFRICA	11	ment, U.S. *Over Seas Loans*
EUROPE	13	*and Grants, Obligations*
NEAR EAST AND SOUTH ASIA	11	*and Loan Authorizations,*
		July 1, 1945 to June 30, 1967,
TOTAL	64	D.C., March 29, 1968.

An important aspect of the new United States leadership position is its direct replacement of other imperialist powers. Eugene V. Rostow, Under Secretary of State for Political Affairs, put it this way in a radio interview: " . . . . in many ways the whole postwar history has been a process of American movement to take over positions . . . . of security which Britain, France, the Netherlands and Belgium had previously held."[32]

Nor has United States business been caught napping while all this has been going on. For example, United States banks abroad are no longer concentrated mainly in Latin America, but are now spread out over the globe. And the United States position in the lush Middle East oil industry has been transformed. Table 2 presents estimates of the change in the relative position of the United States with respect to Middle East oil. While United States firms controlled less than 10 percent of the reserves in Middle Eastern oil leases before the Second World War and 72 percent was held by Great Britain, the positions are now reversed: the United States now controls almost 59 percent while the British share has fallen to a little more than 29 percent. The reasons for this reversal are

not to be sought in the greater ingenuity or ability of the United States oil industry but rather in the politics of the Middle East, the uses of United States Lend
Lease during the Second World War, postwar foreign aid programs, and the
ingenuity of the State Department and other government agencies.[33]

TABLE 2   *Oil Reserves in Middles East —Estimates of*
                    Reserves Controlled (The amounts are in billions of barrels)

	1940		1967	
	Amount	*% of Total*	*Amount*	*% of Total*
GREAT BRITAIN	4.3	72.0	73.0	29.3
UNITED STATES	0.6	9.8	146.0	58.6
OTHER	1.1	18.2	30.0	12.1
TOTAL	6.0	100.0	249.0	100.0

Source: 1940. Based on data from Zuhayr Mikdashi, *A Financial Analysis of Middle Eastern Oil Concessions* (New York: Praeger, 1966).

Source: 1967. Based on data from *Oil and Gas Journal*, December 25, 1967. These
data are estimates , based on the assumptions that the oil reserves in a country are
owned by major concessionaires. If anything, this assumption results in an under-
estimation of the U.S. share in 1967 as compared with Great Britain.

3) The new technology, spurred on by the war, is much more international in
scope than the older technology, and therefore has special implications for the
current and future operation of imperialism. The most obvious aspect is the
technology of space. The large number of "space" stations around the globe
manned by United States technicians is one of the international features.
Another is the preeminent role of the United States in communications satel-
lites, so that not only *Life, Readers' Digest, Time,* Hollywood movies, and the
publications of the United States Information Agency are on hand, but United
States television fare is instantly available: all useful means for attaining a "cultural" unity which mirrors the United States guidance of the imperialist system.
With this have also come new international legal arrangements, as noted by Secretary Rusk: "And to start building a single global communications satellite sys-

tem, we have created a novel international institution in which a private Ameri-can corporation shares ownership with 45 governments."[34]

In addition, the technologies of atomic energy and computers have special international features. The enormous investment in research and development required for these industries gives a special edge to the corporations which are large enough to be multinational in scale. Without trying to trace the causal inter-connections, we should be aware of the happy blending of the new technology and the international corporation: a) The United States has firms which are large enough to have, or be able to obtain, sufficient capital to develop the necessary technology and take advantage of preempting the field in other countries. b) Unit-ed States firms are supported in this technical lead by huge government grants of research and development. c) These same firms have had experience in interna-tional operations, either on their own or in cooperation with the United States government in the process of the latter's stretching its various military and foreign aid activities around the globe. d) Along with generous government assistance has come an integrated apparatus of scientific research and technical development in the large corporation, one result of which is the considerable reduction of the lead time between scientific advances and the introduction of new products, thus giv-ing the international corporation a global edge over smaller and less powerful rivals. Finally, e) the technological advances embodied in the jet plane have made more feasible the coordinated management of the multinational corporation.

Demand for External Sources of Raw Materials

ONE OF THE FEATURES of imperialism that persists unabated to this day is the reliance of the giant corporation for its monopolistic position, including the size of its profits, on foreign sources of raw materials. What is new in today's imperialism is that the United States has become a "have-not" nation for a wide range of both common and rare minerals.

A strange sort of reasoning crops up these days in academic discussions of this subject because advanced industrialized countries are importing a smaller value of raw materials in proportion to output of final products than in the past. This trend reflects increasing efficiency in the industrial uses of raw materials resulting from: 1) improvements in technology and design; 2) increased com-plexity of consumer products (that is, more manufacturing work is applied to a given amount of raw materials); 3) development of synthetic materials (rubber, plastics, fibers); and 4) improved organization of scrap collection and utilization.

This increasing efficiency in raw materials use is undoubtedly important. It has a serious bearing on the prosperity and viability of the underdeveloped primary commodity producing countries. It is an important contributor to the differential rates of growth between the industrialized and non-industrialized countries. It is involved in the increasing financial dependency of many underdeveloped economies, which will be discussed below. But a strange leap in reasoning is needed to conclude that the strategic role of raw materials has changed for the advanced countries. No matter how efficient industry becomes in the use of aluminum or in the extraction of alumina from bauxite, you can't make aluminum without bauxite and you can't make an airplane without aluminum. And when in the United States 80 to 90 percent of the bauxite supply comes from foreign sources, the assurance of such supply is of crucial importance to the aluminum industry, the airplane industry, and the country's military power.

Another factor often cited as tending to minimize the raw materials problem is the technical achievements in the processing of low-grade ores, and the use of substitute materials (e.g. plastics for metals). Significant technical strides have indeed been made but, as the data we are about to present will show, these achievements have not reversed the trend. With all the amazing accomplishments of scientists and the wonders of electronics and atomic energy, they still have not discovered how to make ordinary metals behave, except within narrow limits, according to the will of the user.

What may seem dramatic in the laboratory or in a pilot plant is often a far cry from what is needed in practice to transform an entire industry. Managers of business may plan for the future, but they live in the present. Any president of a big corporation who did not aggressively pursue acquisition of foreign leases for raw materials because in the historical long run a domestic substitute will probably be found, would most properly be fired from his job.

Thinking in terms of national planning (for the good of the people) or in abstract economic analysis (in terms of cost curves) does not help to understand the impact of foreign raw materials supplies on the policies of business and government. The question boils down to the nature of control and behavior in business, and the government's realistic response to the operational needs of business. Thus, great developments in the exploitation and use of shale oil, which may some day eliminate domestic dependency on foreign sources, do not and will not diminish the rivalry among oil firms to acquire every bit of oil under land or sea they can lay their hands on. The decisive issues are not consumer and social needs but the controls business firms desire in order to manage world production and prices for the sake of greater profits.

While monopolistic behavior patterns produce the eager drive for foreign supply sources, the shift of the United States from a "have" to a "have-not" nation has likewise resulted in an intensification of the urgency to obtain and control foreign resources. The central point for minerals industries is shown in Table 3. As can be seen from the last column of this table, up until the 1920's, the United States was a net exporter of minerals; the change in trend is postponed by the depression when consumption of raw material declined. The situation, however, reverses significantly during the war years. But the new situation faced by the United States, simultaneous with its new role as organizer and leader of the imperialist network, shows up dramatically in the 1950s, when in place of its former position as a net exporter, close to 13 percent of domestic consumption is supplied by imports.

TABLE 3   *Minerals: Net Imports Compared with Consumption**
Annual Averages in Millions of 1954 Dollars

Period	Imports	Exports	Net Imports**	Apparent Domestic Consumption	Net Imports As percent of Consumption**
1900–1909	$323	$374	$–51	$3,313	–1.5%
1919–1919	534	694	–160	5,135	–3.1
1920–1929	915	863	52	7,025	0.7
1930–1939	792	749	43	6,812	0.6
1940–1944	1,494	922	572	10,802	5.3
1945–1949	1,653	990	663	12,064	5.5
1950–1960	3,103	1,026	2,077	16,170	12.8
1961	3,647	1,145	2,502	17,894	14.0

* All minerals except gold.

** A minus sign means that exports were larger than imports.

Source: U.S. Bureau of the Census. Working Paper No. 6, "Raw Materials in the United States Economy: 1900–1961 (Washington, D.C., 1963.)

This change did not occur because of the growing need to import esoteric materials not found in the United States. On the contrary, the reason was the rapid jump in imports of the more common materials which traditionally were abundant in this country. This can be seen in Table 4, where a comparison is made between net imports of six garden-variety minerals and the domestic extraction of these materials: the situation today is compared with the prewar years.

TABLE 4   *Selected Minerals: Net Imports As a Percent of*
Domestic Mine or Well Production

	1937–39 *Average percentages*	1966 *percentages*	
IRON ORE	3	43	*Source*: 1937– 1940. Calculated from data in U.S. Bureau of the Census, 1937–39. *Statistical Abstract of the United States*: 1939, Washington, D.C. and ibid, 1940. *Source*: 1966. Calculated from data in U.S. Department of Interior, *Minerals Yearbook*, 1966, Washington, D.C. 1967.
COPPER	–13	18	
LEAD	0	131	
ZINC	7	140	
BAUXITE	133	638	
PETROLEUM	–4	31	

Net Imports equals imports minus exports.

Note: These data do not deal with total consumption. The latter includes refining from scrap and use of inventories. This tables only represents the change in dependency on imports as compared with use of domestic natural resources.

Note especially the data on iron ore. Back in the years just before the war, net imports of iron ore amounted to about 3 percent of the close to 52 million tons of iron ore extracted from domestic sources. In 1966, net imports were equal to 43 percent of the 90 million tons mined in the country. (The latter includes the mining of such taconite as we have learned and choose to use productively.) The exhaustion of high-quality domestic ore supplies occasioned a dramatic rise in foreign investment to develop more efficient and richer sources of iron ore in Canada, Venezuela, Brazil, and Africa. The purpose, as it developed, was not only to exploit more profitable sources of supply but to map out greater control over this essential raw material as a preventive measure: each large domestic producer naturally anticipates similar moves by other domestic and foreign producers.

It is true that in recent years technical innovations have increased the utility of domestic ores. Nevertheless, the tendency to increasing reliance on foreign sources of supply persists, partly to get one's money's worth out of an investment already made, partly as a protective device to keep the lesser quality ore sources in reserve, and partly for immediate financial advantage where foreign ores are more economical. As specialists in the field see it, in the absence of a further breakthrough in technology that would make the very low grade iron ore, derived from taconite and similar rock, decidedly cheaper than foreign ore, the prognosis is for increased reliance of our steel industry on foreign sources of ore. Thus, it is anticipated that about half of the iron ore to be consumed in 1980 will be met by foreign sources, and that by 2000 the import ratio will reach 75 percent.[35]

The dramatic reversal in the self-sufficiency of the United States with respect to raw materials was succinctly summarized in a report by the staff of the President's Commission on Foreign Economic Policy:

> This transition of the United States from a position of relative self-sufficiency to one of increasing dependence upon foreign sources of supply constitutes one of the striking economic changes of our time. The outbreak of World War II marked the major turning point of this change.
>
> Both from the viewpoint of our long-term economic growth and the viewpoint of our national defense, the shift of the United States from the position of a net exporter of metals and minerals to that of a net importer is of overshadowing significance in shaping our foreign economic policies.
>
> We have always been almost entirely dependent on imports for tin, nickel, and the platinum group of metals. In addition, our requirements for asbestos, chromite, graphite, manganese, mercury, mica, and tungsten have been generally covered by imports. Prior to World War II this was about the extent of our list of strategic materials, that is mineral substances of which our requirements are wholly or substantially supplied by foreign sources. At present, by contrast, *the United States is fully self-sufficient only in coal, sulfur, potash, molybdenum and magnesium.* (Emphasis added.)[36]

Strategic Materials

THE DEFENSE DEPARTMENT operates with a list of strategic and critical materials as a guide to the stockpiling program. These are the materials which are assumed to be critical to the war potential of this country and where supply difficulties can be anticipated. However, war products are not the only ones for which these materials are strategic. Many civilian products in today's technical environment rely on the same materials. (Mica, for example, appears on this list. Mica is used in the electrical industry in condensers, telephones, dynamos, and in electric toasters.) The import dependency of these materials is shown in Table 5. For more than half of these items, 80 to 100 percent of the supply in this country depends on imports.

TABLE 5   *Classification of Strategic Industrial Materials*
                                     by Degree of Dependence on Imports

Number of Materials	Ratio of Imports To New Supply (Percent)	Source: Percy W. Bidwell, Raw Materials, New York, Harper & Bros., 1958, p. 12.
38	80–100	
6	60–79	
8	40–59	
3	20–39	
7	Less than 20	
62		

For 52 out of the 62 materials, at least 40 percent has to be supplied from abroad. And, according to a report of the International Development Advisory Board (a special commission set up by the President in the 1950s), *three quarters of the imported materials included in the stockpile program come from the underdeveloped areas.* The political and military response to this fact is clearly formulated by the President's Board: ". . . it is to these countries that we must look for the bulk of any possible increase in these supplies. The loss of any of these materials, through aggression, would be the equivalent of a grave military set-back."[37]

The jet engine, the gas turbine, and nuclear reactors are having an important influence on demand for materials which can only be obtained from abroad. The nature of this new need was spelled out in the report of the President's Material Policy Commission:

> The advent of the gas turbine and jets for fighter aircraft, and the possible development for commercial flying and later for automobiles, has accentuated the need for materials to withstand high temperature and stress. One reason why it

has taken so long to develop the gas turbine commercially is that there were no materials that could withstand red heat and at the same time take the stress of the centrifugal forces generated by 20,000 revolutions per minute. Since in the gas turbine the higher the temperature, the greater the efficiency, there is urgent need for metals, ceramics, or other substances that can operate under stress in the range above 2,000 degrees Fahrenheit.

There are also requirements for materials for carrying out nuclear reactions, many of which occur at high temperatures. Some of these materials must have a low capacity for neutron absorption as well. Thus, the need for higher and ever higher temperature resistance becomes one of our most critical problems.[38]

What this means can be seen quite clearly when we narrow our focus on one product—the jet engine, which since this report was prepared has become a commercial as well as military means of transportation. Table 6 lists the six critical materials which are needed to make a jet engine. Except for molybdenum, we are dependent on imports for an adequate supply of all these items. For three of the materials, the dependence is complete. In the last column are listed the current main producers of each product in the non-Communist world. In parentheses after each country is given the percentage its output represents of total production in the non-Communist world.

TABLE 6   *Critical Materials Used for Jet Engine*

	Pounds Used in Jet Engine[1]	*Imports as % of Consumption*[2]	*Where this Material is Produced*[3]
Tungsten	80 – 100	24%	U.S. (30%), South Korea(19%), Canada (12%), Australia (8%), Bolivia (8%), Portugal (7%)
Columbium	10 – 12	100%	Brazil (54%), Canada (21%), Mozambique (18%)
Nickel	1,300 – 1,600	75%	Canada (71%), New Caledonia (20%)
Chromium	2,500 – 2,800	100%	South Africa (31%), Turkey (19%), South Rhodesia (19%), Philippines (18%), Iran (5%)

Molybdenum	90 – 100	0	U.S. (79%), Canada (10%), Chile (9%)
Cobalt	30 – 40	100%	Congo (Leopoldville) (60%), Morocco(13%), Canada (12%), Zambia (11%)

1   From Percy W. Bidwell, *Raw Materials* (New York: Harper & Bros., 1958), p. 12.
2   Calculated from data in U.S. Department of Interior, *Minerals Year Book, 1996*, (Washington, D.C., 1967).
3   Major producers of the material in the non-Communist world. The percentages in parenthesis represent the amount produced in the country in 1966 as a percentage of total production in non-Communist countries. The source for this information is the same as 2.

The facts presented here are of course no mystery to business or to the government planners and coordinators of policy. President Truman established in 1951 the Materials Policy Commission, cited above, to study the materials problem of the United States and its relation to other non-Communist countries. The resulting five-volume report was issued with much publicity in the midst of the Korean War. The theme of raw materials sources as an ingredient of foreign policy crops up not only with respect to direct United States requirements but also as it concerns United States responsibility as the leader of the "free world" to see to it that Western Europe's and Japan's supplies of raw materials are assured. Consider, for example, this frank statement by former President Eisenhower:

> One of Japan's greatest opportunities for increased trade lies in a free and developing Southeast Asia .... The great need in one country is for raw materials, in the other country for manufactured goods. The two regions complement each other markedly. By strengthening of Vietnam and helping insure the safety of the South Pacific and Southeast Asia, we gradually develop the great trade potential between this region .... and highly industrialized Japan to the benefit of both. In this way freedom in the Western Pacific will be greatly strengthened.[39]

And finally, two more citations—one from the Republican side and one from the Democratic side of policy making. The Rockefeller Brothers Fund report on foreign economic policy offers these propositions:

Europe's economic security today depends on two indispensable factors: 1) her own intellectual and technical vitality and economic enterprise; and 2) an international structure which will enable Europe to have access to foreign markets on fair terms and adequate supplies of materials, if Europe can offer reasonable value in return for them.

Nevertheless, the economic situation of the industrialized nations remains precarious. If Asia, Middle Eastern and African nationalism, exploited by the Soviet bloc, becomes a destructive force, European supplies of oil and other essential raw materials may be jeopardized.[40]

W. W. Rostow, President Johnson's closest adviser on national security affairs, seems to be well aware of the underpinning of the imperialist network as it applies to raw materials and to the special role of the United States in today's imperialism. Testifying before the Joint Congressional Committee, Rostow explained the relations between industrialized and underdeveloped nations as follows:

The location, natural resources, and populations of the underdeveloped areas are such that, should they become effectively attached to the Communist bloc, the United States would become the second power in the world. . . . Indirectly, the evolution of the underdeveloped areas is likely to determine the fate of Western Europe and Japan and, therefore, the effectiveness of those industrialized regions in the free world alliance we are committed to lead. If the underdeveloped areas fall under Communist domination, or if they move to fixed hostility to the West, the economic and military strength of Western Europe and Japan will be diminished, the British Commonwealth as it is now organized will disintegrate, and the Atlantic world will become, at best, an awkward alliance, incapable of exercising effective influence outside a limited orbit, with the balance of the world's power lost to it. In short, our military security and our way of life as well as the fate of Western Europe and Japan are at stake in the evolution of the underdeveloped areas. We evidently have a major national interest, then, in developing a free world coalition which embraces in reasonable harmony and unity the industrialized states of Western Europe and Japan on the one hand, the underdeveloped areas of Asia, the Middle East, and Africa, on the other.[41]

United States as the Leading Capital Exporter

Along with the political and military changes after the Second World War, when the United States assumed the role of undisputed leader of world capitalism, came the clear-cut preeminence of the United States as a capital exporter. While the urgent need to develop foreign raw material sources contributed to the momentum of capital exports after the war, the acceleration of investment in foreign manufacturing ventures added a new dimension to the internationalization of capital. To appreciate better this new feature, let us first examine the competitive aspects of world trade in manufactures. Table 7 presents estimates of the shares of five industrial nations in world export trade in manufactures. Aside from the remarkable change in Italy's fortunes during the last two decades, and the rise of Japan's trade, the most noteworthy changes over the practically 70 years covered is the juxtaposition of the United States and the United Kingdom. Britain's share of world trade in manufactures declined from 33 to 12 percent, while that of the United States increased from 12 to 21 percent. But note also that the United States was not able to maintain the lead it took right after the war: between 1950 and 1967, the United States share declined from almost 27 to almost 21 percent, about the same as its share after the First World War.

TABLE 7   *Share of Exports of Manufactured Goods (in percentage)*

	1899	1913	1929	1937	1950	1967
UNITED STATES	11.7	13.0	20.4	19.2	26.6	20.6
UNITED KINGDOM	33.2	30.2	22.4	20.9	24.6	11.9
GERMANY	22.4	26.6	20.5	21.8	7.0*	19.7*
FRANCE	14.4	12.1	10.9	5.8	9.6	.5
ITALY	3.6	3.3	3.7	3.5	3.6	7.0
JAPAN	1.5	2.3	3.9	6.9	3.4	9.9
OTHERS	13.2	12.5	18.2	21.9	25.2	22.4
TOTAL	100.0	100.0	100.0	100.0	100.0	100.0

* West Germany only. A comparable figure for West Germany alone, in 1937, is estimated at 16.5%.

Source: A. Maizels, *Industrial Growth and World Trade*, Cambridge, England, 1963—except for the 1967 data. (Data for 1899 and 1913 exclude the Netherlands.) 1967 data: National Institute, *Economic Review*, February, 1968.

However, isolating just these figures is deceptive. For beginning with the First World War, and at an accelerated pace after the Second World War, a major share of the competitive struggle for markets was taken over by building factories or buying up businesses abroad. The new situation in this respect is presented in Table 8. This table shows the relative position of leading capital exporters at the time of the First World War, at the end of the boom of the 1920's, and in 1960. During the initial period shown on this table, the United Kingdom was the outstanding foreign investor: half of external capital investments were owned by British citizens. Despite the fact that the United States was a debtor nation until after the First World War, it had already started to get its feet wet in this field, beginning with the onset of its participation in the imperialist way of life.

TABLE 8   *Foreign Investments of Leading Capital Exporting Countries (precent of total)*

	1914	1930	1960	
UNITED KINGDOM	50.3	43.8	24.5	*Source*: Calculated
FRANCE	22.2	8.4	4.7*	from data in William
GERMANY	17.3	2.6	1.1	Woodruff, *Impact*
NETHERLANDS	3.1	5.5	4.2*	*of Western Man,*
SWEDEN	0.3	1.3	0.9*	New York, 1966,
UNITED STATES	6.3	35.3	59.1	p. 150, except for the
CANADA	0.5	3.1	5.5	items with asterisk.
TOTAL	100.0	100.0	100.0	

* The data for 1960 are very broad estimates, made solely to simplify the presentation on the relative change of the U.S. position.

The interwar years, and the consequent change in position to that of a creditor nation, gave the United States its opportunity and it raced ahead to the point where it was getting close to the position of the oldest and best entrenched capital exporter. By 1960, United States foreign investments accounted for almost 60 percent of the world total. (These data apply to both portfolio and direct investment. Direct investment—the ownership of branches and subsidiaries— was the most important factor in this expansion of United States investment.

Hence, if the data were shown for direct investment alone, the United States share would be even larger. While all the information is not available for the post-1960 period, it seems clear that the United States share has kept on increasing in these years as well.)

Because of this huge expansion of investment in manufacturing industries abroad, the United States is able to compete in foreign markets directly rather than by exports alone. What this means can be seen from the data in Table 9 for the years 1957 and 1965, the latest year for which such information is presently available. The first three columns show the sales experience of United States firms abroad (branches or subsidiaries of United States corporations). The last three columns report the amount of exports from the United States for the same industries.

TABLE 9   *Exports and Sales from Foreign Investments (Millions)*

Selected Manufactured Industries	Sales of Foreign Affiliates			Exports from U.S.		
	1957	*1965*	*Increase*	*1957*	*1965*	*Increase*
Paper & Allied Products	$881	$1,820	$939	$223	$389	$166
Chemicals	2,411	6,851	4,440	1,457	2,402	945
Rubber Products	968	1,650	682	161	167	6
Metals	1,548	3,357	1,809	1,881	1,735	–146
Non-Electrical Machinery	1,903	5,257	3,354	3,102	5,158	2,056
Electrical Machinery & Equipment	2,047	3,946	1,899	874	1,661	787
Transportation Equipment	4,228	10,760	6,532	1,784	3,196	1,412

Source: Sale of Foreign Affiliates—*Survey of Current Business*, Nov., 1966; Exports—U.S. Bureau of Census, *Statistical Abstract of the United States*, 1966 and ibid.: 1965

It is especially noteworthy that in all the industries, by 1965, the sales of foreign affiliates are higher than exports from United States based plants. More than that, the increase during these years has been larger in the case of foreign affiliates plants than in exports. For the industries combined, sales of foreign-owned plants rose 14 percent, while exports from the United States went up 55 percent.

Sales from manufacturing firms abroad assist in the penetration of foreign markets in a double way. Not only do they obtain a share of the market in the country in which the subsidiary is located, but they enter into the foreign trade channels of the competing powers. This can be seen by an examination of Table 10. Thus, United States plants located in Europe sell only 77 percent of their output to the local markets in which the plants are located. Exports to other countries account for 22 percent of the sales of these plants. Note the relatively small percentage of exports from the underdeveloped world (Latin America and other), the significance of which will be pointed out later when we discuss the issue of financial dependency of underdeveloped countries.

TABLE 10   *Manufacturing Sales Abroad by Foreign Affiliates*
                            of U.S. Firms (Percent of total sales abroad)

	Canada	Latin America	Europe	Other
LOCAL SALES	81	93	77	92
TO U.S.	11	2	1	2
TO OTHER COUNTRIES	8	5	22	6
TOTAL	100	100	100	100

Source: Calculated from data in *Survey of Current Business*, November, 1966.

The impact of these overseas sales from direct investment is what was no doubt in the mind of the investment banker who wrote in a recent article in *Foreign Affairs*:

The role of U.S. direct investment in the world economy is staggering. According to the U.S. Council of the International Chamber of Commerce, the gross value of production by American companies abroad is well in excess of $100 billion a year That is to say, on the basis of the gross value of their output, U.S. enterprises abroad in the aggregate comprise the third largest country (if such a term can be used to designate these companies) in the world—with a gross product greater than that of any country except the United States and the Soviet Union. Of course, these enterprises are large users of raw materials and components produced locally, so that their contribution to the net product (values added) is much less than their gross sales.[42]

As far as manufacturing is concerned, the huge foreign business operation is mainly concentrated in Canada and Europe, as can be seen from Table 11. And since the Second World War, in an environment influenced by the Marshall Plan and NATO, the trend has been the flow of manufacturing capital to Europe.[43]

TABLE 11   *Direct Foreign Investment in Manufacturing (Million $)*

	1950		1966	
	Dollars	*Percent of Total*	*Dollars*	*Percent of Total*
All Areas	$3,831	100%	$22,050	100%
Selected Areas				
Canada	1,897	49.5	7,674	34.8
Mexico	133	3.5	797	3.6
Argentina	161	4.2	652	3.0
Brazil	285	7.4	846	3.8
Europe	932	24.3	8,879	40.3
South Africa	44	1.1	271	1.2
India	16	0.4	118	0.5
Japan	5	0.1	333	1.5
Philippines	23	0.6	180	0.8
Australia	98	2.6	999	4.5

Source: Department of Commerce, *United States Business Investment in Foreign Countries*, Washington, D.C., 1960, and Walther Lederer and Frederick Cutler, International Investments of the United States in 1966 in *Survey of Current Business*, September, 1967.

But the United States is not the only contender for these markets. The cross currents of investment, as a reflection of the competition among giant corporations for markets, is shown in Table 12. English firms invest in France and West Germany. Belgium invests in France, West Germany, and England. Obviously, however, the position of the United States as a foreign investor in Europe is overwhelming. As might be expected, the concentration of investment by a small number of giant firms has resulted in the United States firms' having quite impressive shares of the market in particular industries in Europe. Observe from Table 13 that United States firms control over half of the automobile industry in Britain, close to 40 percent of petroleum in Germany, and over 40 percent of the telegraphic, telephone, electronic, and statistical equipment business in France (the control of computing machines in France is 75 percent).

TABLE 12   *The American Share in the Stock of Foreign Investment*

	France 1962	West Germany 1964	Britain 1962
UNITED STATES	45%	34%	72%
GREAT BRITAIN	12	10	—
NETHERLANDS	11	17	2
SWITZERLAND	5	16	7
BELGIUM	8	5	1
FRANCE	—	7	2
SWEDEN	1	3	1
ITALY	5	*included in others*	1
WEST GERMANY	3	—	1
CANADA	2	*included in others*	9
OTHERS	8	8	4
TOTAL	100%	100%	100%

Source: Christopher Layton, *Trans-Atlantic Investments* (Boulogne-sur-Seine, France: The Atlantic Institute, 1966), p. 13.

TABLE 13   *Estimates of U.S. Share in Certain Industries*

France 1963   *U.S. Firms (percent of sale)*

Petroleum refining	20%	Lifts & elevators	30
Razor blades & safety razors	87	Tractors & agricultural machinery	35
Cars	13	Telegraphic & telephone equipment	42
Tires	*over* 30	Electronic & statistical machines	43
Carbon black	95	(of which computers 75)	
Refrigerators	25	Sewing machines	70
Machine tools	20	Electric razors	60
Semi-conductors	25	Accounting machines	75
Washing machines	27		

Britain 1964   *U.S. Firms (percent of sale)*

Petroleum products	*over* 40%	Pharmaceuticals	*over* 20
Computers	*over* 40	Agricultural machinery	*over* 40
Cars	*over* 50	Instruments	*over* 15
Carbon black	*over* 75	Safety razors/blades	*approx.* 55
Refrigerators	33 1/3 % to 50		

West Germany		U.S. Firms (percent of sale)	
Petroleum	38%	Chemicals, rubber, etc.	3
Machinery, vehicles, metal		Electrical, optics, toys, musical	
products (of which cars 40%)	15	(of which computers 84%)	10
Food Industry	7		

Source: Christopher Layton, *Trans-Atlantic Investments* (Boulogne-sur-Seine, France: The Atlantic Institute. 1966), p. 19.

The tie-in between monopolistic trends and the flow of investment to Europe is indicated by the following; in "the three biggest European markets (West Germany, Britain, and France) 40 percent of United States direct investment is accounted for by three firms—Esso, General Motors, and Ford. In all Western Europe, 20 United States firms account for two thirds of United States investment.[44] Between 1950 and 1965 "more and more of the major companies have bought or built their way into Europe. By 1961, 460 of the 1000 largest U.S. companies had a subsidiary or branch in Europe. By 1965, the figure had risen to 700 out of 1000."[45]

In short, the internationalization of capital among the giant firms is of a much higher order today than was the case fifty years ago when Lenin wrote his work on imperialism.

3.   The American Empire and
the U.S. Economy

THREE INTERRELATED VIEWS on economic imperialism and United
States foreign policy prevail today:

1) Economic imperialism is not at the root of United States foreign policy.
   Instead, political aims and national security are the prime motivators of
   foreign policy.

2) Economic imperialism cannot be the main element in foreign policy determination, since United States foreign trade and foreign investment make such
   relatively small contributions to the nation's overall economic performance.

3) Since foreign economic involvement is relatively unimportant to the United
   States economy, it follows that economic imperialism need not be a moti-
   vating force in foreign policy. Hence some liberal and left critics argue that
   present foreign policy, to the extent that it is influenced by imperialism, is
   misguided and in conflict with the best economic interests of this country. If
   we sincerely encouraged social and economic development abroad, the
   argument goes, even to the extent of financing the nationalization of United
   States foreign investment, the rising demand for capital imports by underdeveloped countries would create a more substantial and lasting stimulus to
   prosperity than the current volume of foreign trade and foreign investment.

Obscuring economic and commercial interests by covering them up or inter-
mingling them with idealistic and religious motivations is hardly a new phenomenon. Wars have been fought to impose Christianity on heathen empires—
wars which incidentally also opened up new trade routes or established new

centers of commercial monopoly. Even such a crass commercial aggression as
the Opium War in China was explained to the United States public by the
American Board of Commissioners for Foreign Missions as "not so much an
opium or an English affair, as the result of a great design of Providence to make
the wickedness of men subserve his purposes of mercy toward China, in breaking through her wall of exclusion, and bringing the empire into more immediate contact with Western and Christian nations."[1]

John Quincy Adams, in a public lecture on the Opium War, explained that
China's trade policy was contrary to the law of nature and Christian principles:

> The moral obligation of commercial intercourse between nations is founded
> entirely, exclusively, upon the Christian precept to love your neighbor as yourself.
> . . . But China, not being a Christian nation, its inhabitants do not consider them-
> selves bound by the Christian precept, to love their neighbor as themselves. . . .
> This is a churlish and unsocial system. . . . The fundamental principle of the Chi-
> nese Empire is anti-commercial. . . . It admits no obligation to hold commercial
> intercourse with others. . . . It is time that this enormous outrage upon the rights of
> human nature, and upon the first principles of the rights of nations, should cease.[2]

Perhaps the Christian principle of "love thy neighbor" and the more modern
ethic that the anti-commercial is also immoral have become so habitual in
accepted ways of thought that we have lost the facility to separate the various
strands that make up foreign policy. Perhaps the source of the difficulty can be
traced to a lack of understanding of what Bernard Baruch called "the essential
one-ness of [United States] economic, political and strategic interests."[3]

There will probably be little dispute about the "one-ness" of United States
political and national security aims. The only rationale of national security today
is "defense" against the Soviet Union and China. To be absolutely safe, it is said,
we need also to cope with the "concealed wars" which may appear as internal revolutions or civil war.[4] It is merely coincidental, to be sure, that socialist revolutions
destroy the institutions of private ownership of the means of production and
thereby violate the Christian precept to love thy neighbor by eliminating freedom
of trade and freedom of enterprise in large and important sectors of the earth.

The "one-ness" of the political and national security aims becomes more
evident on examination of the political aims, since in this realm of thought our
policy-makers and policy-defenders are strict economic determinists. Political
freedom is equated with Western-style democracy. The economic basis of this

democracy is free enterprise. Hence the political aim of defense of the free world must also involve the defense of free trade and free enterprise. The primary departure from this rigid economic determinism appears when dealing with politically unstable nations where, obviously, the art of self- government is not fully developed. In such cases, for the sake of political stability, we permit and encourage military dictatorships, in full confidence that the people of these countries will eventually learn the art of self-government and adopt a free society just so long as the proper underpinning of free enterprise remains. While our policy-makers and policy-defenders will identify in the most general terms the "one-ness" of the nation's foreign political and national security goals, they usually become quite shy when it comes to the question of the unity of these goals and economic interests. We have come a long way from the very straightforward bulletin prepared in 1922 by the Office of Naval Intelligence on "The U.S. Navy as an Industrial Asset."[5] This report frankly details the services rendered by the Navy in protecting American business interests and in seeking out commercial and investment opportunities which the Navy Department brings to the attention of American businessmen.

But today our national aims are presumably concerned only with political and philosophic ideals. In so far as economic interests are concerned, the tables have been turned: today it is business that is expected to serve the needs of national policy. The problem is how to stimulate private investment abroad. Private foreign investment is considered such a necessary tool of national policy that various forms of investment guaranty programs have been designed to protect foreign investors against losses due to confiscation, wars, and the uncertainties of currency convertibility.

The interrelation between economic interests and foreign policy is seen more dearly by business-minded observers. Thus the former president and chairman of the World Bank, Eugene R. Black, informs us that "our foreign aid programs constitute a distinct benefit to American business. The three major benefits are: 1) Foreign aid provides a substantial and immediate market for U.S. goods and services. 2) Foreign aid stimulates the development of new overseas markets for U.S. companies. 3) Foreign aid orients national economies toward a free enterprise system in which U.S. firms can prosper."[6]

More specifically, an Assistant Secretary of Commerce for Economic Affairs explains to businessmen that "if these [military and economic] aid programs were discontinued, private investments might be a waste because it would not be safe enough for you to make them."[7]

On a much more elevated plane, we are told by a specialist on international business practice, a teacher at MIT and Harvard: "It would seem that there is a horrible urgency in making Western economic concepts internationally viable if man's dignity is to be preserved—and incidentally, a profitable private business."[8]

And as an indication of how in fact some influential members of the business community see the "one-ness" of economic, political, and security interests, listen to the view expressed in 1965 by the Vice-President of Chase Manhattan Bank who supervises Far Eastern operations:

> In the past, foreign investors have been somewhat wary of the over-all political prospect for the [Southeast Asia] region. I must say, though, that the U.S. actions in Vietnam this year—which have demonstrated that the U.S. will continue to give effective protection to the free nations of the region—have considerably reassured both Asian and Western investors. In fact, I see some reason for hope that the same sort of economic growth may take place in the free economies of Asia that took place in Europe after the Truman Doctrine and after NATO provided a protective shield. The same thing also took place in Japan after the U.S. intervention in Korea removed investor doubts.[9]

The Size of Foreign Economic Involvement

BUT EVEN IF WE GRANT the interrelatedness of economic, political, and security interests, how much priority should we assign to economic interests? Specifically, how can one claim that economic imperialism plays a major role in United States policy if total exports are less than 5 percent of the gross national product, and foreign investment much less than 10 percent of domestic capital investment?

Let us note first that the size of ratios is not by itself an adequate indicator of what motivates foreign policy. Many wars and military operations were aimed at control over China's markets at a time when those markets represented only one percent of total world trade. Overall percentages need analytical examination: the strategic and policy- influential areas of business activity need to be sorted out. Above all, it is important to appreciate that the stake of United States business abroad is many times larger than the volume of merchandise exports. The reason for this is that the volume of accumulated capital abroad controlled by United States business has been increasing at a faster rate than exports. The unique advantage of capital is that it reproduces itself. That is, the output obtained by capital investment produces enough revenue to cover not only costs of labor and raw materials but also the capital and natural resources consumed plus profits. The annual flow of capital invested abroad is therefore additive: increments to capital enlarge the productive base. Even more important, United States firms abroad are able to mobilize foreign capital for their operations. The net result of the flow of capital abroad and the foreign capital mobilized by American firms is that while production abroad arising out of United States investment was 4_ times larger than exports in 1950, by 1964 this had risen to 5_ times exports. These observations are based on estimates made in a recent study conducted by the National Industrial Conference Board[10] (see table).

TABLE 14   *Output abroad resulting from U.S. investment*

| | Sales (in billions) | |
	1950	1964
From direct investment	$24	$88
From other investment	20	55
TOTAL	44	143
Sales abroad via exports	10	25
Total output abroad plus exports	$54	$168

When the Department of Commerce measures the economic significance of exports, it compares them with a figure for total domestic production of moveable goods—that is, the sales of agricultural products, mining products, manufactures, and freight receipts. The estimated total of moveable goods produced in the United States in 1964 was $280 billion.[11] There are technical reasons which make it improper to compare the $168 billion of sales abroad with $280 billion of domestic output of moveable goods. For example, a portion of our exports is shipped to United States–owned companies as components or semi-finished products. Thus, if we add such exports to output of United States–owned foreign business we are double counting. Adjusting for this and other sources of non- comparability, we arrive at a conservative estimate that the size of the foreign market (for domestic and United States–owned foreign firms) is equal to approximately two-fifths the domestic output of farms, factories, and mines.[12]

If this seems surprising to those who are accustomed to think in terms of Gross National Product, remember that the latter includes government expenditures, personal and professional services, trade, and activities of banks, real estate firms, and stock brokers. But as far as the business of farms, factories, and mines is concerned, foreign business amounts to quite a noteworthy volume relative to the internal market. Nor is this the whole story. These data do not include the considerable amount of sales abroad of foreign firms operating under copyright and patent agreements arranged by United States firms. As an example, one firm in the Philippines manufactures the following brand-name products under restricted licenses of United States firms: "Crayola" crayons, "Wessco" paints, "Old Town" carbon paper and typewriter ribbons, "Mongol" lead pencils, "Universal" paints, and "Parker Quink."

The Growing Importance of Foreign Economic Activity

THE INCREASING relative importance of foreign economic activity is well illustrated by the experience of the manufacturing industries, as shown in Chart I and Table 29. Here we compare total sales of domestic manufactures with exports of manufactures and sales of United States direct investments in foreign manufacturing activity. The data are plotted on a semi-logarithmic scale in the chart. Therefore, the narrowing of the distance between the two lines depicts the more rapid rise of the foreign market as compared with the growth of domestic markets.

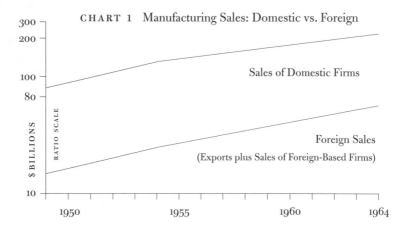

CHART 1   Manufacturing Sales: Domestic vs. Foreign

Sales of Domestic Firms

Foreign Sales
(Exports plus Sales of Foreign-Based Firms)

TABLE 15   *Manufactures Foreign and Domestic Sales (in billions)*

1	2	3	4		5	
Year	*Exports*	*Sales by Foreign-based U.S. Firms*	*Total Foreign Sales 2) + 3)*		*Sales of Domestic Manufactures*	
			Absolute	*1950–100*	*Absolute*	*1950–100*
1950	$ 7.4	$ 8.4	$15.8	100	89.8	100
1955	12.6	13.9	26.5	168	135.0	150
1960	16.1	23.6	39.7	251	164.0	183
1964	20.6	37.3	57.9	367	203.0	226

Source: Exports—U.S. Bureau of the Census, *Statistical Abstract of the United States*: 1965, pp. 877, 773. 1964 Sales of Domestic firms—U.S. Bureau of the Census, *Annual Survey of Manufactures*, 1964. Sales of foreign-based U.S. firms—the data for 1950 and 1955 are estimates based on the average relation between sales and investment abroad. (This is the procedure used by the National Industrial Conference Board.) Data for 1960 and 1964—*Survey of Current Business*, September 1962, p. 23, November 1965, p. 18.

Note: The data in columns 4) and 5) are not strictly comparable (see note 12). However, the non-comparability does not destroy the validity of comparing the differences in the rates of growth of the two series.

CHART 2   Plant and Equipment Expenditures of Manufacturing Firms

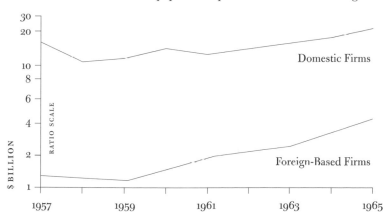

Equally significant is the comparison of expenditures for plant and equipment in foreign-based and in domestic manufacturing firms (Chart 2 and Table 17). As in the preceding chart, the narrowing of the distance between the two lines is a clear portrayal of the increasing relative importance of business activity abroad. Expenditures for plant and equipment for United States subsidiaries abroad were a little over 8 percent of such expenditures of domestic firms in 1957. Last year this had risen to 17 percent.

TABLE 16   *Plant and Equipment Expenditures by U.S. Domestic*
and Foreign-Based Manufacturing Firms

| Year | Domestic Firms | | Foreign-Band Firms | | Foreign as % |
	Billion $	1957=100	Billion $	1957=100	of Domestic
1957	$16.0	100.0	$1.3	100	81.0
1958	11.4	71	1.2	92	10.5
1959	12.1	76	1.1	85	9.1
1960	14.5	91	1.4	108	9.7
1961	13.7	86	1.8	139	13.1
1962	14.7	92	2.0	154	13.6
1963	15.7	98	2.3	177	14.7
1964	18.6	116	3.0	231	16.1
1965	22.5	141	3.9	300	17.3

Source: Foreign-based firms—*Survey of Current Business*, September 1965, p. 28; September 1966, p. 30. Domestic firms—*Economic Report of the President*, (Washington, D.C., 1966), p. 251.

It is not surprising to find, as shown in Chart 3 and Table 17, that profits from operations abroad are also becoming an ever more important component of business profits. In 1950, earnings on foreign investment represented about 10 percent of all after- tax profits of domestic nonfinancial corporations. By 1964, foreign sources of earnings accounted for about 22 percent of domestic nonfinancial corporate profits. In evaluating the significance of this we should also take into account a) the understatement of foreign earnings because the latter do not include all the service payments transferred by foreign subsidiaries to home corporations, and b) the financial advantages achieved in allocating costs between the home firms and foreign subsidiaries so as to minimize taxes.

Moreover, we are comparing foreign earnings with earnings of all nonfinancial corporations—those that are purely domestic and those that operate abroad as well as in the United States. If we compared foreign earnings with total earnings of only those industries that operate abroad, the share of foreign earnings would of course be much larger than one fourth.

TABLE 17   *Earnings on Foreign Investments and DomesticCorporate Profits (Billions of dollars)*

	Earnings on Foreign Investment	Profits (After Taxes) of Domestic Nonfinancial Corporations
1950	2.1	21.7
1951	2.6	18.1
1952	2.7	16.0
1953	2.6	16.4
1954	2.8	16.3
1955	3.3	22.2
1956	3.8	22.1
1957	4.2	20.9
1958	3.7	17.5
1959	4.1	22.5
1960	4.7	20.6
1961	5.4	20.5
1962	5.9	23.9
1963	6.3	26.2
1964	7.1	31.3
1965	7.8	36.1

Source: Earnings on foreign investments—U.S. Department of Commerce, Balance of Payments Statistical Supplement, Revised Edition (Washington, 1963); Survey of Current Business, August 1962, August 1963, August 1964, September 1965, June 1966, September 1966. Profits of nonfinancial domestic corporations—Survey of Current Business, September 1965, July 1966.

Note: Earnings include a) earnings on direct investment abroad, b) fees and royalties on direct investment transferred to parent companies in the U.S., and c) income from "other investments (other than direct) transferred to U.S. owners of these assets.

The significance of the last three tables is their representation of the rapid growth of the foreign sector. During the period when the economy as a whole was experiencing a slowing down in the rate of growth, foreign markets were an important source of expansion. For example, in manufacturing industries during the past ten years domestic sales increased by 50 percent, while foreign sales by United States–owned factories increased over 110 percent.

CHART 3   Plant and Equipment Expenditures of Manufacturing Firms

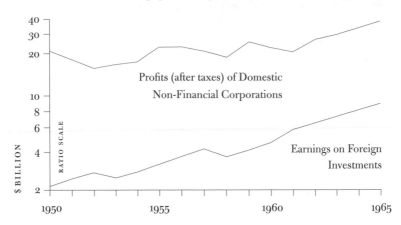

Thus, as far as the commodity-producing industries are concerned, foreign markets have become a major sphere of economic interest and have proven to be increasingly important to United States business as an offset to the stagnating tendencies of the inner markets.

This is quite obvious to American businessmen. The treasurer of General Electric Company put it this way in discussing "the need that American business has to keep expanding its foreign operations":

> In this respect, I think business has reached a point in the road from which there is no turning back. American industry's marvelous technology and abundant capital resources have enabled us to produce the most remarkable run of peacetime prosperity in the nation's history. To keep this going, we have for several years sought additional outlets for these sources in foreign markets. For many companies, including General Electric, these offshore markets offer the most promising opportunities for expansion that we can see.[13]

It is also quite obvious that if foreign markets arc so important to the commodity- producing industries, they are also of prime importance to the other interest groups, those whose profits and prosperity are dependent upon the welfare of the commodity-producers as well as those who benefit from servicing trade and investment in foreign markets: investment and commercial bankers, stock market speculators, transportation, insurance, etc.

Military Spending and Exports

FOR A FULL MEASURE of economic involvement in foreign markets, the impact of military spending—the "defense" program—must also be reckoned with. The growth of our inner and outer markets has, since the founding of the Republic, been associated with the use (actual or threatened) of military force in peace as well as war. Professor William T. R. Fox states the case quite mildly:

> The United States Army in peacetime was through most of the nineteenth century, extensively used to aid in the winning of the West, and especially in the suppression of Indian opposition to the opening up of new lands for settlement. Our Navy and Marine Corps, beginning with their exploits against the Barbary pirates were also engaged in making it safe for Americans to live and invest in remote places.[14]

While military activity is today presumably subordinated to national security needs, the "one-ness" of the national security and business interests persists: the size of the "free" world and the degree of its "security" define the geographic boundaries where capital is relatively free to invest and trade. The widespread military bases, the far-flung military activities, and the accompanying complex of expenditures at home and abroad serve many purposes of special interest to the business community: 1) protecting present and potential sources of raw materials; 2) safeguarding foreign markets and foreign investments; 3) conserving commercial sea and air routes; 4) preserving spheres of influence where United States business gets a competitive edge for investment and trade; 5) creating new foreign customers and investment opportunities via foreign military and economic aid; and, more generally, 6) maintaining the structure of world capitalist markets not only directly for the United States but also for its junior partners among the industrialized nations, countries in which United States business is becoming ever more closely enmeshed. But even all of this does not exhaust the "one-ness" of business interest and military activity, for we need to take into account the stake business has in the size and nature of military expenditures as a well-spring of new orders and profits.

As with exports, the significance of military spending for business and the economy as a whole is usually greatly underestimated. One often hears that defense expenditures amount to less than 10 percent of the Gross National Product and that with a proper political environment comparable government spending for peaceful uses could accomplish as much for the economy. A crucial weakness of this approach is its uncritical acceptance of Gross National Product as a thing-in-itself. Because GNP is a useful statistical tool and one which has become entrenched in our ways of thought, we tend to ignore the underlying strategic relationships that determine the direction and degree of movement of the economic aggregates. Instead of examining the requirements of the industrial structure and the dynamic elements of economic behavior, we tend to view the economy as blocks of billions of dollars that may be shifted at will from one column to another of the several categories used by statisticians to construct the measurement of GNP.

To appreciate fully the critical influence of foreign markets and military expenditures on the domestic economy, recognition must be given to their exceptionally large impact on the capital goods industries. But first a comment on the capital goods industries and the business cycle. There are diverse explanations of business cycles, but there can be no disputing the fact that the mechanics of the business cycle—the transmission mechanism, if you wish—is to be found in the ups and downs of the investment goods industries. There are cycles which are primarily related to the ebb and flow of inventories, but these are usually short-lived as long as the demand for investment goods does not collapse.

During a cyclical decline, the demand for consumer goods can be sustained for a period by several expedients such as unemployment relief, other welfare payments, and depletion of consumer savings. However, except for the most essential replacement needs, expenditures on investment goods theoretically can go down to zero. Businessmen naturally will not invest unless they expect to make a profit. The result of the diverse behavior of producer goods and consumer goods was classically demonstrated in the depression of the 1930's. During this probably worst depression in our history, purchases of consumer goods declined only 19 percent (between 1929 and 1933). Compare this with the behavior of the two major types of investment goods during the same period: expenditures for residential construction fell by 80 percent and nonresidential fixed investment dropped 71 percent.

With this as background, let us now focus on the post–Second World War relationship between a) exports and military demand, and b) a major category of investment, non-residential fixed investment goods. Table 18 lists the industries producing nonresidential investment goods. It should be noted that a number of these industries also contribute to consumer goods (e.g., steel and machinery for autos) and to residential construction. This table presents the

TABLE 18 *Percent of Total Output Attributable to Exports and Federal Purchases, 1958*

INDUSTRY	Going into Exports	Purchased by Federal Government	Total of Exports and Federal Purchases
Iron and ferroalloy ores mining	13.5%	12.8%	26.3%
Nonferrous metal ores mining	9.1	35.6	44.7
Coal mining	19.1	6.3	25.4
Ordnance and accessories	1.7	86.7	88.4
Primary iron and steel manufacturing	10.1	12.5	22.6
Primary nonferrous metal manufacturing	10.1	22.3	32.4
Stamping, screw machine products	7.1	18.2	25.3
Other fabricated metal products	8.6	11.9	20.5
Engines and turbines	14.8	19.7	34.5
Farm machinery and equipment	10.0	2.9	12.9
Construction, mining and oil field machinery	26.9	6.1	33.0
Materials handling machinery and equipment	9.4	17.2	26.6
Metalworking machinery and equipment	14.0	20.6	34.6
Special industry machinery and equipment	17.5	4.3	21.8
General industrial machinery and equipment	13.4	15.3	28.7
Machine shop products	7.0	39.0	46.0
Electric industrial equipment and apparatus	9.8	17.0	26.8
Electric lighting and wiring equipment	5.5	14.5	20.0
Radio, TV and communication equipment	4.8	40.7	45.5
Electronic components and accessories	7.6	38.9	46.5
Misc. electrical machinery, equipment and supplies	8.9	15.1	24.0
Aircraft and parts	6.1	86.7	92.8
Other transportation equipment (not autos)	10.1	20.9	31.0
Scientific and controlling instruments	7.3	30.2	37.5

Source: "The Interindustry Structure of the United States," *Survey of Current Business*, November 1964, p. 14.

percentages of total demand (direct and indirect) created by exports and purchases of the federal government, which are almost entirely for military needs. These data are for the year 1958, the latest year for which there exists a complete input-output analysis for the United States economy.

As will be noted from Table 18, in only one industry—farm machinery and equipment—did the combined export and military demand come to less than 20 percent of total demand. At the opposite extreme are the military industries par excellence—ordnance and aircraft. For all the other industries, the range of support given in 1958 by exports and military demand is from 20 to 50 percent.

While the available statistical data refer to only one year, the postwar patterns of exports and military expenditures suggest that this tabulation is a fair representation of the situation since the Korean War, and surely a gross underestimate during the Vietnam War. More information and study are required for a more thorough analysis. Meanwhile, the available data warrant, in my opinion, these observations:

1) Exports and military spending exert a distinctive influence on the economy because they fortify a strategic center of the existing industrial structure. This is especially noteworthy because business investment is not, as is too often conceived, a freely flowing stream. There is a definite interdependence between a) the existing schedule of wage rates, prices, and profits, b) the evolved structure of industry (the types of interrelated industries, each built to be profitable at the scale of obtainable domestic and foreign markets), and c) the direction of profitable new investments. To put it in simpler terms, there are sound business reasons why investments flow in the direction they do and not in such ways as to meet the potential needs of this country—for example, to eliminate poverty, to provide the industry which would create equal opportunity to Negroes, to develop the underdeveloped regions of the United States, or create adequate housing. More important, business cannot invest to accomplish these ends and at the same time meet its necessary standards of profit, growth, and security for invested capital. Exports of capital goods and military demand flowing to the capital-goods producers, on the other hand, are uniquely advantageous in that they strengthen and make more profitable the established investment structure; they also contribute to an expansion of the industries that are most harmonious with and most profitable for the existing composition of capital.

2) The support given by foreign economic involvement—both military and civilian commodities—makes a singular contribution by acting as a bulwark against the slippage of minor recessions into major depressions. It has accomplished this by shoring up one of the strategic balance wheels of the economy, the production of investment-type equipment—by supplying, as we have seen, from 20 to 50 percent of the market for these goods.

3) We need also to take into account that it is monopolistic industry which dominates the volume and flow of investment and that such monopolistic businesses characteristically gear their investment policies to the "sure thing," where good profits and safety of investment are reliably assured. Here the tie-in of government action and foreign policy is of paramount interest. The military-goods market usually has the decided advantage of supplying long-term contracts, often accompanied by enough guarantees to reduce and even eliminate any risk in building additional plant equipment, plant and equipment which may also be used for civilian purposes. In addition, military contracts pay for related research and development expenses, again removing risky aspects of normal investment programs. As for the foreign countries, the United States military presence, its foreign policy, and its national security commitments provide a valuable protective apparatus for the investments made in foreign markets. These foreign investments, together with the demand created by governmental foreign aid, contribute importantly to the demand for the exports of the capital-goods and other manufacturing industries. The confidence in the consistency of government foreign policy and its complementary military policy can, and surely must, act as a valuable frame of reference for the domestic as well as foreign investment practices of monopolistic business.

4) The extra 20 to 50 percent of business provided by exports plus military demand (as shown for the key industries in Table 17) provides a much greater percentage of the total profits of these firms. The typical economics of a manufacturing business requires that a firm reaches a certain level of productive activity before it can make a profit. Gross overhead costs—depreciation of machinery, use of plant, costs of administration—remain fairly constant at a given level of capacity. Until production reaches a point where at the market price of the final product enough income is produced to meet the overhead and direct costs, a business operates at a loss. Once this "break-

even" point is reached, the profitability of the business surges forward until it hits against the limits of productive capacity. Of course the curve of profitability differs from industry to industry and from firm to firm. But the existence of a break-even point, and the upward swing of profits after the break-even point has been passed, is a common characteristic of manufacturing industries. What this means is that for many of the firms in the capital goods industries, the overlay of 20 to 50 percent of demand from military purchases and exports probably accounts for the major share of the profits, and in not a few firms perhaps as much as 80 to 100 percent of their profits.

Monopoly and Foreign Investments

ONE OF THE REASONS frequently given for believing that economic imperialism is an unimportant influence in foreign and military policy is that only a small segment of American business is vitally concerned with foreign or military economic activities. This might be a meaningful observation if economic resources were widely distributed and the majority of domestic-minded business firms could conceivably be mobilized against policies fostered by the small minority of foreign-oriented businesses. But the realities of economic concentration suggest quite the opposite. In manufacturing industries, 5 corporations own over 15 percent of total net capital assets (as of 1962). The 100 largest corporations own 55 percent of total net capital assets.[15] This means that a small number of firms—with their own strength and that of their allies in finance and mass communication media—can wield an overwhelming amount of economic and political power, especially if there is a community of interest within this relatively small group.

And it is precisely among the giant corporations that we find the main centers of foreign and military economic operations. Just a cursory examination of the 50 largest industrial concerns shows the following types of firms heavily involved in international economic operations and the supply of military goods: 12 in oil, 5 in aviation, 3 in chemicals, 3 in steel, 3 in autos, 8 in electrical equipment and electronics, and 3 in rubber. These 37 companies account for over 90 percent of the assets of the top 50 industrial firms.

The community of interest among the industrial giants in foreign and military operations stems from relations that are not always obvious in terms of the customary statistical categories. First, there is the interrelationship among the firms via the financial centers of power. Second, there are the direct economic ties of business. While only five firms get one fourth of the volume of military contracts and 25 firms account for more than half of such contracts, a large part of this business is distributed to other businesses that supply these chief contractors.[16] Thus, as we saw in Table 18 the primary nonferrous metal manufacturers who receive very few direct military contracts nevertheless get over 22 percent of their business from military demand. And, third, because of the rich growth potential and other advantages of the military and foreign- oriented businesses, the postwar merger movement among industrial giants has intermingled the typically domestic with the typically outer-market directed business organizations. The most unlikely-seeming business organizations are today planted with both feet in foreign and military business. We see, for example, traditional producers of grain mill products and of plumbing and heating equipment acquiring plants that make scientific instruments, meat packing firms buying up companies in the general industrial machinery field, and many other cross-industry mergers.

TABLE 19   *U.S. Direct Foreign Investment by*
                                          Size of Investment (1957)

Value of Direct Investment by Size Classes	*Number of Firms*	*Percent of Total U.S. Investment*	
			Source: United States Business Investments in Foreign Countries,
$ 100 million *and over*	45	57	
$ 50-100 million	51	14	U.S. Dept. of
$ 25-50 million	67	9	Commerce, 1960,
$ 10-25 million	126	8	p. 144.
$ 5-10 million	166	5	

The concentration of economic power, so much part of the domestic scene, shows up in even stronger fashion in the field of foreign investment. The basic available data on this are taken from the 1957 Census of foreign investments. (See table below.) These data refer only to direct investments and do not include portfolio investments or such economic ties as are created by the licensing of patents, processes, and trademarks. We note from this table that only 45 firms account for almost three fifths of all direct foreign investment. Eighty percent of all such investment is held by 163 firms. The evidence is still more striking when we examine the concentration of investment by industry:

TABLE 20   *Holdings by Industry*

Industry	Number of Firms	Percent of Total Assets Held
Mining	20	95
Oil	24	93
Manufacturing	143	81
Public Utilities	12	89
Trade	18	83
Finance and Insurance	23	76
Agriculture	6	83

These data are shown from the viewpoint of total United States foreign invest-ment. If we examined the situation from the angle of the recipient countries, we would find an even higher degree of concentration of United States business activities. But from either perspective, the concentration of foreign investment is but an extension of domestic monopolistic trends. The latter provide the opportunity to accumulate the wealth needed for extensive foreign investment as well as the impetus for such investment.

The question of control is central to an understanding of the strategic factors that determine the pattern of foreign investment. In its starkest form, this control is most obvious in the economic relations with the underdeveloped countries— in the role of these countries as suppliers of raw materials for mass-production industries and as a source of what can properly be termed financial tribute.

Let us look first at the distribution of foreign investment as shown in Table 21. We see here two distinct patterns. In Latin America, Asia, and Africa, the majority of the investment is in the extractive industries. Although Canada is an important source of minerals and oil, only 35 percent of United States ininvest-ment is in these extractive industries, with 45 percent going into manufactures. The investment in extractive industries in Europe is minimal: the data on petro-leum represent refineries and distribution, not oil wells.

The economic control, and hence the political control when dealing with foreign sources of raw material supplies, is of paramount importance to the monopoly-organized mass production industries in the home country. In indus-tries such as steel, aluminum, and oil, the ability to control the source of raw material is essential to the control over the markets and prices of the final products, and serves as an effective safety factor in protecting the large investment in the manufacture and distribution of the final product. The resulting frustration of competition takes on two forms. First, when price and distribution of the raw material are controlled, the competitor's freedom of action is restricted; he cannot live very long without a dependable source of raw materials at a practical cost. Second, by gobbling up as much of the world's resources of this material as is feasible, a power group can forestall a weaker competitor from becoming more independent as well as discourage possible new competition. How convenient that a limited number of United States oil companies control two thirds of the "free world's" oil![17]

TABLE 21   *Percent Distribution of Direct Foreign Investment*
                      by Area and Industry, 1964

Industry	All Areas	Canada	Europe	Latin America	Africa	Asia	Oceania
Mining	8.0%	12.1%	0.4%	12.9%	21.9%	1.1%	6.3%
Petroleum	32.4	23.4	25.6	35.9	51.0	65.8	28.1
Manufacturing	38.0	44.8	54.3	24.3	13.8	17.5	54.1
Public Utilities	4.6	3.3	0.4	5.8	0.1	1.8	0.1
Trade	8.4	5.8	12.2	10.7	5.7	7.8	5.5
Other	8.6	10.6	7.1	10.7	7.5	6.0	5.9
TOTAL	100.0	100.0	100.0	100.0	100.0	100.0	100.0

At this level of monopoly, the involvement of business interests with United States foreign policy becomes ever more close. The assurance of control over raw materials in most areas involves not just another business matter but is high on the agenda of maintaining industrial and financial power. And the wielders of this power, if they are to remain in the saddle, must use every effort to make sure that these sources of supply are always available on the most favorable terms: these foreign supplies are not merely an avenue to great profits but are the insurance policy on the monopolistic position at home.

The pressure to obtain external sources of raw materials has taken on a new dimension during the past two decades, and promises to become increasingly severe. Even though United States business has always had to rely on foreign sources for a number of important metals (e.g., bauxite, chrome, nickel, manganese, tungsten, tin), it has nevertheless been self-reliant and an exporter of a wide range of raw materials until quite recently. This generalization has been a mainstay of those who argued that U.S. capitalism had no need to be imperialistic. But even this argument, weak as it may have been in the past, can no longer be relied on. The developing pressure on natural resources, especially evident since the 1940's, stirred President Truman to establish a Materials Policy Commission to define the magnitude of the problem. The ensuing commission report, Resources for Freedom (Washington, D.C., 1952), graphically summarized the dramatic change in the following comparison for all raw materials other than food and gold: at the turn of the century, the U.S. produced on the whole some 15 percent more of these raw materials than was domestically consumed; this surplus had by 1950 turned into a deficit, with U.S. industry consuming 10 percent more than domestic production; extending the trends to 1975 showed that by then the overall deficit of raw materials for industry will be about 20 percent.

Perhaps the awareness of this development was a contributing factor to President Eisenhower's alerting the nation to the unity of political and economic interests in his first inaugural address (January 20, 1953):

> We know . . . that we are linked to all free peoples not merely by a noble idea but by a simple need. No free people can for long cling to any privilege or enjoy any safety in economic solitude. For all our own material might, even we need markets in the world for the surpluses of our farms and our factories. Equally, we need for these same farms and factories vital materials and products of distant lands. This basic law of interdependence, so manifest in the commerce of peace, applies with thousand-fold intensity in the event of war.

As is so often the case, economic interests harmonize comfortably with political and security goals, since so many of the basic raw materials are considered essential to effective war preparedness. Quite understandably the government makes its contribution to the security of the nation as well as to the security of business via diplomatic maneuvers, maintenance of convenient military bases in various parts of the world, military aid to help maintain stable governments, and last but not least a foreign aid program which is a fine blend of declared humanitarian aims about industrialization and a realistic appreciation that such progress should not interfere with the ability of supplying countries to maintain a proper flow of raw materials. To do a real job of assuring an adequate supply of raw materials in the light of possible exhaustion of already exploited deposits, and in view of possible needs for missiles and space programs, the government can make its greatest contribution by keeping as much of the world as possible "free" and safe for mineral development. Clarence B. Randall, president of Inland Steel Co. and adviser on foreign aid in Washington, comments on the fortunate availability of uranium deposits in the Belgian Congo as the atom bomb was developed: "What a break it was for us that the mother country was on our side! And who can possibly foresee today which of the vast unexplored areas of the world may likewise possess some unique deposit of a rare raw material which in the fullness of time our industry or our defense program may most urgently need?"[18]

The integration of less developed capitalisms into the world market as reliable and continuous suppliers of their natural resources results, with rare exceptions, in a continuous dependency on the centers of monopoly control that is sanctified and cemented by the market structure which evolves from this very dependency. Integration into world capitalist markets has almost uniform effects on the supplying countries: 1) they depart from, or never enter, the paths of development that require independence and self-reliance; 2) they lose their economic self-sufficiency and become dependent on exports for their economic viability; 3) their industrial structure becomes adapted to the needs of supplying specialized exports at prices acceptable to the buyers, reducing thereby such flexibility of productive resources as is needed for a diversified and growing economic productivity. The familiar symptom of this process is still seen in Latin America where, despite industrialization efforts and the stimulus of two world wars, well over 90 percent of most countries' total exports consists of the export of agricultural and mineral products.[19] The extreme dependence on exports, and on a severely restricted number of export products at that, keeps such economies off balance in their international economic relations and creates frequent need for borrowing. Debt engenders increasing debt, for the servicing of the debt adds additional balance of payments difficulties. And in all such relations of borrowing and lending, the channels of international finance are in the hands of the foreign investors, their business associates, and their government agencies.

The chains of dependence may be manipulated by the political, financial, and military arms of the centers of empire, with the help of the Marines, military bases, bribery, CIA operations, financial maneuvers, and the like. But the material basis of this dependence is an industrial and financial structure which through the so-called normal operations of the marketplace reproduces the conditions of economic dependence.

A critical element of the market patterns which helps perpetuate the under-developed countries as dependable suppliers of raw materials is the financial tribute to the foreign owners who extract not only natural resources but hand-some profits as well. The following comparison for the years 1950–1965 is a clear illustration of the process and refers to only one kind of financial drain, the income from direct investments which is transferred to the United States:[20]

TABLE 22   *Billions of Dollars*

	Europe	Canada	Latin America	All other Areas
Flow of direct investments from U.S.	$8.1	$6.8	$3.8	$5.2
Income on this capital transferred to U.S.	5.5	5.9	11.3	14.3
NET	+$2.6	+$ .9	-$7.5	-$9.1

In the underdeveloped regions almost three times as much money was taken out as was put in. And note well that besides drawing out almost three times as much as they put in, investors were able to increase the value of the assets owned in these regions manyfold: in Latin America, direct investments owned by United States business during this period increased from $4.5 billion to $10.3 billion; in Asia and Africa, from $1.3 billion to $4.7 billion.

The contrasting pattern in the flow of funds to and from Europe indicates a post–Second World War trend. The rapid growth of investment in Europe was in the manufacturing and oil refining fields. The developments in foreign invest-ment in manufacturing are closely related to the normal business drive to a) con-trol markets and b) minimize costs of production. The methods used will vary according to the industry and the conditions in each country. The main factors involved in relying on capital investment instead of relying on export trade are:

1) If the profit rate obtainable by manufacturing abroad is greater than by increasing domestic production.

2) If it facilitates getting a larger and more secure share of a given foreign market.

3) If it enables taking advantage of the channels of export trade of the country in which investment is made. Thus, United States business firms in England account for 10 percent of Britain's exports.[21]

4) If it is possible to pre-empt a field of industry based on new technological developments, usually protected by exercise of patent rights. But the most dramatic development of our times is the spread of United States industry into the computer, atomic energy, and space technology activities of industrialized countries. The rapid spread of these fields is motivated, to be sure, by immediate profit opportunities. But it most likely also has the aim of helping to maintain, and get full advantage of, the technical edge United States business now has as a result of the vast investment made by the United States government in research and development. The dominant position in this technology may be decisive in achieving wider control of the rest of the economy, when and if the new technology becomes the key to the productive forces of a society.

Such investment as is made by United States capital in manufacturing in underdeveloped countries occurs primarily in Latin America, where the percentage of total United States investment in the field of manufacturing is 24 percent. This investment is mainly in light manufacturing industry, including the processing of native food materials. Manufacturing operations in the durable goods field, such as autos, takes the form of assembly plants. This guarantees the export market of components and parts. It also contributes to stabilizing the market for these United States products. It is much easier for a country faced with severe balance of payments difficulties to prohibit imports of a luxury product than to eliminate the import of raw materials and assembly parts which will create unemployment and shut down local industry.

The postwar foreign economic expansion of United States manufacturing firms has resulted in the transformation of many of the giants of United States business into a new form of multinational organizations. The typical international business firm is no longer limited to the giant oil company. It is as likely to be a General Motors or a General Electric—with 15 to 20 percent of its operations involved in foreign business, and exercising all efforts to increase this share. It is the professed goal of these international firms to obtain the lowest unit production costs on a world-wide basis. It is also their aim, though not necessarily openly stated, to come out on top in the merger movement in the European

Common Market and to control as large a share of the world market as they do of the United States market. To the directors of such organizations the "one-ness" of economic and national interests is quite apparent. The president of General Electric put it succinctly: "I suggest we will perceive: that overriding both the common purposes and cross-purposes of business and government, there is a broader pattern—a 'consensus' if you will, where public and private interest come together, cooperate, interact and become the national interest."[22]

Needless to stress, the term "private interest" refers to private enterprise. Another officer of this corporation grapples with the identity of the private and national interest: "Thus, our search for profits places us squarely in line with the national policy of stepping up international trade as a means of strengthen-ing the free world in the Cold War confrontation with Communism."[23]

Just as the fight against Communism helps the search for profits, so the search for profits helps the fight against Communism. What more perfect har-mony of interests could be imagined?

4.   Imperialism Without Colonies

THE SUDDEN UPSURGE during the late nineteenth century in the aggressive pursuit of colonies by almost all the great powers is, without doubt, a primary distinguishing trait of the "new imperialism." It is surely the dramatic hallmark of this historic process, and yet it is by no means the essence of the new
imperialism. In fact, the customary identification of imperialism with colonialism is an obstacle to the proper study of the subject, since colonialism existed
before the modern form of imperialism and the latter has outlived colonialism.

While colonialism itself has an ancient history, the colonialism of the last five
centuries is closely associated with the birth and maturation of the capitalist
socioeconomic system. The pursuit and acquisition of colonies (including
political and economic domination, short of colonial ownership) was a
significant attribute of the commercial revolution which contributed to the disintegration of feudalism and the foundation of capitalism. The precapitalist
regional trade patterns around the globe were not destroyed by the inexorable
forces of the market. Instead, it was superior military power that laid the basis
for transforming these traditional trade patterns into a world market centered on
the needs and interests of Western Europe. The leap ahead in naval power—
based on advances in artillery and in sailing vessels able to carry the artillery—
created the bludgeoning force used to annex colonies, open trading ports,
enforce new trading relations, and develop mines and plantations. Based on
mastery of sea power, this colonialism was mainly confined to coastal areas,
except for the Americas where the sparse population had a primitive technology and was highly susceptible to European infectious diseases.[1] Until the nineteenth century, economic relations with these colonies were, from the European
standpoint, import-oriented, largely characterized by the desire of the metropolitan countries to obtain the esoteric goods and riches that could be found

only in the colonies. For most of those years, in fact, the conquering Europeans had little to offer in exchange for the spices and tropical agricultural products they craved, as well as the precious metals from the Americas.

The metropolitan-colonial relation changed under the impact of the Industrial Revolution and the development of the steam railway. With these, the center of interest shifted from imports to exports, resulting in the ruination of native industry, the penetration of large land areas, a new phase in international banking, and increasing opportunity for the export of capital. Still further changes were introduced with the development of large-scale industry based on new metallurgy, the industrial application of organic chemistry, new sources of power, and new means of communication and of ocean transport.

In the light of geographic and historical disparities among colonies and the different purposes they have served at different times, the conclusion can hardly be avoided that attempts such as have been made by some historians and economists to fit all colonialism into a single model are bound to be unsatisfactory. There is, to be sure, a common factor in the various colonial experiences; namely, the exploitation of the colonies for the benefit of the metropolitan centers.[2] Moreover, there is unity in the fact that the considerable changes in the colonial and semicolonial world that did occur were primarily in response to the changing needs of an expanding and technically advancing capitalism. Still, if we want to understand the economics and politics of the colonial world at some point in time, we have to recognize and distinguish the differences associated with the periods of mercantile capitalism, competitive industrial capitalism, and monopoly capitalism, just as we have to distinguish these stages of development in the metropolitan centers themselves if we want to understand the process of capital development.

The identification of imperialism with colonialism obfuscates not only historical variation in colonial-metropolitan relations, but makes it more difficult to evaluate the latest transformation of the capitalist world system, the imperialism of the period of monopoly capitalism. This obfuscation can often be traced to the practice of creating rigid, static, and ahistoric conceptual models to cope with complex, dynamic phenomena. I propose to examine some of the more common misconceptions on which models of this kind are often based in the belief that it will help clarify the theme of imperialism without colonies. Two such misconceptions are particularly common, both of which relate to the vital role played by the export of capital: those based on arguments concerning the export of surplus capital and the falling rate of profit in the advanced capitalist countries.

1. The Pressure of Surplus Capital

A DISTINGUISHING FEATURE of the new imperialism associated with the period of monopoly capitalism (that is, when the giant corporation is in the ascendancy and there is a high degree of economic concentration) is a sharp rise in the export of capital. The tie between the export of capital and imperialist expansion is the obvious need of investors of capital for a safe and friendly environment.

But why the upsurge in the migration of capital during the last quarter of the nineteenth century and its continuation to this day? A frequently-met explanation is that the advanced capitalist nations began to be burdened by a superabundance of capital that could not find profitable investment opportunities at home and therefore sought foreign outlets. While a strong case can be made for the proposition that the growth of monopoly leads to increasing investment difficulties, it does not follow that the export of capital was stimulated primarily by the pressure of a surplus of capital.[3]

The key to answering the question lies, in my opinion, in understanding and viewing capitalism as a world system. The existence of strong nation states and the importance of nationalism tend to obscure the concept of a global capitalist system. Yet the nationalism of capitalist societies is the *alter ego* of the system's internationalism. Successful capitalist classes need the power of nation states not only to develop inner markets and to build adequate infrastructures but also, and equally important, to secure and protect opportunities for foreign commerce and investment in a world of rival nation states. Each capitalist nation wants protection for itself, preferential trade channels, and freedom to operate internationally. Protectionism, a strong military posture, and the drive for external markets are all part of the same package.

The desire and need to operate on a world scale is built into the economics of capitalism. Competitive pressures, technical advances, and recurring imbalances between productive capacity and effective demand create continuous pressures for the expansion of markets. The risks and uncertainties of business, interrelated with the unlimited acquisitive drive for wealth, activate the entrepreneur to accumulate ever greater assets and, in the process, to scour every corner of the earth for new opportunities. What stand in the way, in addition to technical limits of transportation and communication, are the recalcitrance of natives and the rivalry of other capitalist nation states.

Viewed in this way, export of capital, like foreign trade, is a normal function of capitalist enterprise. Moreover, the expansion of capital export is closely

associated with the geographic expansion of capitalism. Back in the earliest days
of mercantile capitalism, capital began to reach out beyond its original borders
to finance plantations and mines in the Americas and Asia. With this came the
growth of overseas banking to finance trade with Europe as well as to help lubri-
cate foreign investment operations. Even though domestic investment opportunities may have lagged in some places and at some times, the primary drive
behind the export of capital was not the pressure of surplus capital but the utilization of capital where profitable opportunities existed, constrained, of
course, by the technology of the time, the economic and political conditions in
the other countries, and the resources of the home country. For example, since
military power was needed to force an entry into many of these profit-making
opportunities, shortages of manpower and economic resources that could readily be devoted to such purposes also limited investment opportunities.

As mentioned above, a reversal in trade relations occurs under the impact of
the Industrial Revolution and the upsurge of mass-produced manufactures.
Capitalist enterprise desperately searches out export markets, while it is the
overseas areas which suffer from a shortage of goods to offer in exchange. As a
result, many of the countries which buy from industrialized countries fall into
debt, since their imports tend to exceed their exports. Under such conditions
opportunities and the need for loan capital from the metropolitan centers
expand. Capital exports thus become an important prop to the export of goods.
As is well known, the real upsurge in demand for British export capital came
with the development of the railway. It was not only British industry that supplied the iron rails and railroad equipment over great stretches of the globe, but
also British loan and equity capital that made the financing of these exports possible. In addition, the financial institutions which evolved in the long history of
international trade and capital export acquired vested interests in the pursuit of
foreign business. Following their own growth imperatives, they sought new
opportunities for the use of capital overseas, while energetically collecting and
stimulating domestic capital for such investments.

The important point is that capital export has a long history. It is a product
of 1) the worldwide operations of the advanced capitalist nations, and 2) the
institutions and economic structure that evolved in the ripening of capitalism as
a world system. It is not the product of surplus capital as such. This does not
mean that there is never a "surplus capital" problem (fed at times by the return
flow of interest and profits from abroad), nor that at times capital will not move
under the pressure of such surpluses. Once sophisticated international money

markets exist, various uses will be made of them. Short-term funds, for instance, will move across borders in response to temporary tightness or ease of money in the several markets. Money will be loaned for more general political and economic purposes, for one country to gain influence and preferential treatment in another. But the main underpinning of the international financial markets is the international network of trade and investment that was generated by the advanced industrial nations in pursuit of their need to operate in world markets. Thus, while surplus domestic capital may at times be a contributing factor to capital movements abroad, the more relevant explanation, in our opinion, is to be found in the interrelations between the domestic economic situation of the advanced capitalist nations and that of their overseas markets.[4]

Why then the sudden upsurge of capital exports associated with modern imperialism? The answer, in my opinion, is consistent with the above analysis as well as with the nature of this later stage of capitalism. First, the onset of the new imperialism is marked by the arrival of several industrial states able to challenge Britain's hegemony over international trade and finance. These other nations expand their capital exports for the same purposes—increased foreign trade and preferential markets. Thus, instead of Britain being the dominant exporter of capital among very few others, a new crop of exporters comes to the fore, with the result that the total flow of capital exports greatly expands. Second, associated with the intensified rivalry of advanced industrial nations is the growth of protective tariff walls: one means of jumping these tariff walls is foreign investment. Third, the new stage of capitalism is based on industries requiring vast new supplies of raw materials, such as oil and ferrous and nonferrous metal ores. This requires not only large sums of capital for exploration and development of foreign sources, but also loan capital to enable foreign countries to construct the needed complementary transportation and public utility facilities. Fourth, the maturation of joint stock companies, the stock market, and other financial institutions provides the means for mobilizing capital more efficiently for use abroad as well as at home. Finally, the development of giant corporations hastens the growth of monopoly. The ability and desire of these corporations to control markets provides another major incentive for the expansion of capital abroad.

The facts on U.S. investment abroad in the present era are quite revealing on the issue of "surplus" capital; they can help us to answer the historical questions as well. One would expect that if a major, if not *the* major, reason for the export of U.S. capital today were the pressure of a superabundance of domestic capital, then as much capital as could be profitably used abroad would be drawn from the United States. But that is not the case. We have the data on the capital structure of U.S. direct investments abroad in the year 1957. (This is the latest year for which such data are available. Another census of foreign investments was taken in 1966, but the results have not yet been published.) What we find is that 60 percent of the direct investment assets of U.S.-based corporations are owned by U.S. residents and 40 percent by non-U.S. residents, mainly local residents, but including overseas European and Canadian capital invested in Latin America, etc. (see Table 23).

Now there is an interesting twist to these data. If we separate equity and debt assets, we discover that U.S. residents own 86 percent of the equity and only 25 percent of the debt. What this reflects is the practice employed by U.S.

firms to assure control over their foreign assets and to capture most of the "perpetual" flow of profits. As for the debt capital (long- and short-term), which in time will be repaid out of the profits of the enterprise, it is just as well to give the native rich a break. The supposedly pressing "surplus" funds of the home country are tapped very little for the debt capital needs of foreign enterprise.

TABLE 23   *U.S. Direct-Investment Enterprise in Other Countries in 1957[1]: Assets Owned by U.S. and Local Residents*

A. *Percentage of total assets in equity and debt*

	TOTAL ASSETS		EQUITY ASSETS		DEBT ASSETS	
	$ billion	*%*	*$ billion*	*%*	*$ billion*	*%*
Owned by U.S.residents	$24.0	100.0	$19.7	82.3	$ 4.2	17.7
Owned by residents[2]	15.6	100.0	3.2	20.6	12.4	79.4
TOTAL	$39.6	100.0	$22.9	58.0	$16.6	42.0

B. *Percentage distribution of assets by U.S. and local ownership*

	TOTAL ASSETS	EQUITY ASSETS	DEBT ASSETS
Owned by U.S.residents	60.5	86.0	25.4
Owned by local residents[2]	39.5	14.0	74.6
TOTAL	100.0	100.0	100.0

1   Finance and insurance investments are excluded.

2 More accurately, non-U.S. residents. The owners are primarily residents of the areas in which U.S. enterprise is located though there was probably a flow of funds from Europe and Canada to U.S.-owned enterprise in other areas.

Source: Calculated from *U.S. Business Investment in Foreign Countries* (Washington, D.C.: U.S. Department of Commerce, 1960).

But we should also be aware that the 60-40 share of the capital assets, mentioned above, exaggerates the capital funds supplied from the United States. Here is how a businessman's publication, *Business Abroad,* describes the overseas investment practices of U.S. corporations:

> In calculating the value of capital investment, General Motors, for example, figures the intangibles such as trademarks, patents, and know- how equivalent to twice the actual invested capital. Some corporations calculate know-how, blueprints, and so on as one third of capital investment, and then supply one third in equity by providing machinery and equipment.[5]

Hence, a good share of the 60 percent of the assets owned by U.S. firms does not represent cash investment but a valuation of their knowledge, trademarks, etc., and their own machinery valued at prices set by the home office.[6]

One may ask whether this phenomenon of using local capital is a feature predominantly of investment practices in wealthier foreign countries. The answer is no. It is true that the share supplied by local capital is larger in European countries (54 percent) and lower in Latin American countries (31 percent), but the practice of obtaining debt capital locally is characteristic of all regions in which U.S. capital is invested (see Table 24).

The facts on the flow of funds to finance U.S. direct investments abroad are even more striking. We have data on the source of funds used to finance these enterprises for the period 1957 to 1965. While this information is for a limited period, other available evidence indicates that there is no reason to consider this period as atypical.[7]

These data reveal that during the period in question some $84 billion were used to finance the expansion and operations of direct foreign investments. Of this total, only a little more than 15 percent came from the United States. The remaining 85 percent was raised outside the United States: 20 percent from locally raised funds and 65 percent from the cash generated by the foreign enterprise operations themselves.

TABLE 24   *Percentage Distribution of Assets of U.S.*
Direct-Investment Enterprises in Other Countries,
by Ownership and Area (in 1957)[1]

Ownership	Total Assets	Equity Assets	Debt Assets
In Canada			
U.S. residents	62.0	78.5	37.2
Local residents[2]	38.0	21.5	62.8
TOTAL	100.0	100.0	100.0
In Europe			
U.S. residents	46.2	83.9	11.1
Local residents[2]	53.8	16.1	88.9
TOTAL	100.0	100.0	100.0
In Latin America			
V.S. residents	69.1	92.9	24.9
Local residents[2]	30.9	7.1	75.1
TOTAL	100.0	100.0	100.0
In Africa			
U.S. residents	51.5	80.7	23.9
Local residents[2]	48.5	19.3	76.1
TOTAL	100.0	100.0	100.0
In Asia			
U.S. residents	62.4	94.1	13.1
Local residents[2]	37.6	5.9	86.9
TOTAL	100.0	100.0	100.0

Source: As for previous table.

TABLE 25   *Sources of Funds of U.S. Direct-Investment Enterprises in Other Countries (1957–1965)*

A. Summary of All Areas

SOURCES OF FUNDS	FUNDS OBTAINED	
	$ billion	*Percent of total*
From United States	$12.8	15.3
Obtained from abroad	16.8	20.1
Obtained form operations of foreign enterprises	54.1	64.6
from net income	33.6	40.1
from depreciation and depletion	20.5	24.5
TOTAL	$83.7	100.0

B. Percentage Distribution, by Area

AREA	PERCENTAGE OF FUNDS OBTAINED		
	From U.S.	*From outside U.S.[1]*	*Total*
Canada	15.7	84.3	100.0
Europe	20.2	79.8	100.0
Latin America	11.4	88.6	100.0
All other areas	13.6	86.4	100.0

1   Includes funds raised abroad from non-U.S. residents and from operations of foreign enterprises.

Source: 1957 data—same as Table 23; 1968-1966 data from *Survey of Current Business*, September 1961; September 1962; November 1965; January 1967.

Here again the pattern is similar for rich countries and poor countries. If anything, the U.S. capital contribution is less in the poor countries than in the rich ones: the U.S. capital contribution is 16 percent for enterprise in Canada, 20 percent in Europe, 11 percent in Latin America, and 14 percent in all other areas. Too many inferences should not be drawn from these differentials; large funds came from the United States during these years to finance the rapid expansion of enterprises in Europe. However, it is proper to observe that only a small percentage of

the supply of funds needed to finance its foreign investments is coming from the
United States. And that is hardly what one would expect on the basis of a theory that the main reason for foreign investment is the pressure of a superabundance of capital at home.

2. The Declining Rate of Profit

A SECOND MAJOR GROUND often advanced for the rise in capital exports is
the declining rate of profit. The reasoning behind this is that capital accumulation,
accompanied by an ever-rising ratio of fixed capital to labor, produces a dominant
tendency for the average rate of profit to decline. Such a decline induces domestic
capitalists to invest abroad where labor costs are lower and profits higher.

We cannot now, and do not need to for this purpose, examine either the internal theoretical consistency of this theory, whether the facts bear it out, or, if it is
true, how this tendency would work under monopoly conditions. This examination is not necessary, in my opinion, because in any case the declining rate of profit
would not explain the pattern of international capital movements. In other words,
it is not a necessary hypothesis in this connection, whether in itself it is true or not.
This point can be substantiated in relation to two types of foreign investment, the
purchase of foreign bonds and the development of oil wells and mines. However,
before presenting my reasons for saying this, I would like to point out that there
are two separate questions. We are concerned here with the *causes* of the export
of capital in the period of imperialism. The *effect* of the export of capital on
domestic profit rates is a different, though undoubtedly important, question.

To return to the pattern of international capital movements. First, the declin-
ing- rate-of-profit hypothesis cannot apply to loan capital. Rates of interest on
money lent abroad are generally attractive, but, for relatively safe loans, they are
considerably below the industrial rate of profit. Thus, a purchase of foreign
bonds by a corporation would not normally be an offsetting action against a
declining rate of profit.

We also need to eliminate this hypothesis to explain the extensive direct
investment in oil extraction and mining. Investments in these industries are not
primarily motivated by comparative profit rates or falling rates of profit at home,
but by the facts of geology. The decisive factors are where the minerals were
placed by God, and the transportation problems of getting them to the consuming centers. Profit rates are, of course, always involved, and they are usually
very high. Also the investor will take advantage of as low wages as he can get

away with. However, the profitability of these extractive industries is not based on low wages but on the abundance of the natural resources where they happen to be and on the monopolistic structures through which they are marketed.

It is true that comparative profit rates do enter the picture when, as in the case of iron mining in the United States, formerly rich iron ore reserves become depleted. A rush then ensues to develop iron reserves in Labrador, Venezuela, and Brazil. But here again the decisive factor is not a declining profit rate due to the process of capitalist accumulation: it is rather a declining profit rate due to the state of nature.

It is a third kind of investment, foreign direct investment in manufacturing, which provides the only real test of the thesis. Here, if anywhere, one might expect capital to flow in response to simple profit-rate differentials. What then about direct investments in manufacturing? It should go without saying that the profit rate dominates all investment decisions, and it should also be clear that capital will continuously seek the highest obtainable profit rate. Whether profit rates are rising or declining at home, we should expect capital to flow out as long as higher profit rates are obtainable abroad. But it is not necessary that profit rates obtainable abroad should be higher than average domestic profit rates to sustain this flow. What concerns the investor is a comparison of the profitability of additional (or marginal) investment in industry at home and industry abroad. Theoretically, the new investment abroad could have a lower return than the average rate of profit at home and still be attractive. For example, assume that a manufacturer of refrigerators is getting a return of 20 percent on his domestic investment. He wants to make a new investment and finds that he will get only 15 percent at home, but that he can get 18 percent if he uses these funds to make refrigerators abroad. He will be prompted to go abroad, with the result that his foreign investments will yield less than his domestic investment. (This is one reason, by the way, why comparisons of data on average manufacturing profit rates at home and abroad are not really meaningful, aside from inadequacies of the statistics themselves.) So it is this gap in marginal profitability which produces the flow of foreign investment; it has no necessary connection with any fall in the average profitability of investment at home.

3. Monopoly and Foreign Investment

A MUCH MORE USEFUL hypothesis than the falling rate of profit, I believe, is one that traces the main drive for direct investment of capital on a global scale to the imperatives of capital operating under monopoly conditions. Such an analytical framework embraces an explanation of 1) the main body of investment, in extractive as well as manufacturing industries, and 2) the stepup in capital exports during the period of imperialism. Its central purpose is to demonstrate the interrelation between the concomitant rise in capital exports and monopoly as the core of the new imperialism.

Business, in general, can best be understood as a system of power, to use a phrase of Robert Brady's. It is of the essence of business to try to control its own market and to operate, so far as possible, as if the entire globe were its preserve. This was true from the very outset of the capitalist era. As long, however, as there were many competitors in most industries, the opportunities for control were quite limited. With the development of monopoly conditions—i.e., when a handful of companies dominates each of the important markets—the exercise of controlling power becomes not only possible but increasingly essential for the security of the firm and its assets.

The emergence of a significant degree of concentration of power does not mean the end of competition. It does mean that competition has been raised to a new level: temporary arrangements among competitors about production, price, and sales policies are more feasible than before, and business decisions can be arrived at with reasonable anticipation of what the competitive response will be. Since capital operates on a world scale, the business arrangements to divide markets and/or the competitive struggle among the giants for markets stretch over large sections of the globe.

Furthermore, the competitive strategy changes from the period of competition. Price-cutting is no longer the preferred method of acquiring a larger share of the market. Prices are kept high, and the expansion of production is restrained by the limitation of effective demand at high prices or the ability to win a larger share of the high-priced market from a competitor. Nevertheless, the necessity to grow persists and the capital available for growth mounts; hence the constant pressure for rivals to get a larger share of each other's markets wherever they may be. It should be noted that this struggle for larger markets will naturally take place in the more developed countries, where markets for sophisticated products already exist and where it is possible to take advantage of the privileged trade channels of each other's colonial or semicolonial empire. This struggle also takes place in the less developed countries, where new markets, however small, can be entered and where the first firms to get a foothold often have lasting advantage.

The impetus to invest abroad arises out of this competitive struggle among the giants. First, the ownership of raw material supplies is of strategic importance in the push for control over prices, to hold one's own against competitors who also control supplies, and to restrict the growth of competitors who do not have their own sources. Second, the need to control and expand markets is a major spur and incentive for capital export, especially where tariffs or other barriers to trade impede the expansion of commodity exports.

The correlation between monopolistic motives and the spread of foreign investment is supported not only by this analysis but by the actual pattern of investment, at least in the case of the largest foreign investor, the United States. The monopolistic aspects of U.S. (and other) investments in oil and metal ores are too well known to need dwelling on here. In manufacturing, it is clear, overseas investment is a game for the larger firms. Thus, in 1962, 94 percent of the assets of U.S. foreign manufacturing corporations were controlled by firms with assets of $50 million or more.[8] Moreover, a study of the 1957 census of U.S. foreign investment showed that the bulk of manufacturing investments were made by oligopolistic firms in areas where the advantages of monopoly can be carried abroad: operations protected by patents, exclusive or advanced technical knowledge, and/or product differentiation through brand identification and similar techniques.[9]

This argument in no way denies the primacy of the profit motive. The whole purpose of monopoly control is to assure the existence and growth of profits. The profit motive and capitalism are, after all, one and the same. What needs explanation is why, with the profit motive always present, the export of capital in the form of direct investment accelerates with the onset of the imperialist stage. Here I suggest that tracing the answer to the nature and mushrooming of monopoly (or, more accurately, oligopoly) is a more meaningful explanation than that provided by the falling-rate-of-profit theory, or, as discussed above, the pressure-of-surplus-capital theory.

Given a chance to make additional profit abroad at a higher marginal rate, the entrepreneur will grab at it, providing the politics of the foreign country is friendly to foreign investment and to the withdrawal of profits from that country. There are, however, many factors that influence the size of the profit margin. Low wages and cost of raw materials are only two of these elements; transportation expenses, productivity of labor, managerial ability, and overhead costs are also significant. And monopolistic or semi-monopolistic influences which protect sales quotas at high prices carry enormous weight. In this context, it should be noted that the investment decisions may be tempered by additional considerations. The fact that a major company has established a beachhead in foreign markets will spur competitors to follow suit: even when the immediate profit gain may not be clearly favorable the longer-run requirements of assuring one's share of the world market dictates such a strategy. And, as noted above, trade restrictions will motivate a firm to invest abroad to protect its market on the other side of the trade barrier. When the balance of ingredients is favorable to the profit and/or market strategy, the decision to invest abroad follows as a matter of course.

While on this subject it may be worth noting that one of the most common of the oversimplified explanations of the transnational movement of capital is that which assigns the decisive role to wage differentials between the capital-exporting and capital- importing countries. For the United States, where wages are relatively high, *any* export of capital could be interpreted this way. But one should not infer from this that the main current of foreign investment is to substitute foreign-made for domestic-made goods on the U.S. market. At best, one might argue that some of the overseas production takes the place of what would otherwise be exports from the United States. (In this fashion, wage differentials are eliminated as a competitive element in overseas markets.) The facts on the distribution of sales of U.S. manufacturing firms located abroad (from 1962 to 1965) show that, except for Canada, less than 2 percent of U.S. production abroad is sent to the United States (see Table 26). The high percentage for Canada consists largely of manufactures based on Canadian resources (paper, for example).

TABLE 26   *Direction of Sales of U.S. Manufacturing Affiliates Located Outside of United States, 1962–1965*

	Percentage distribution			
AREA	Total Sales	Local Sales	Exported to U.S.	Exported to Other Countries
Total	100.0	82.3	4.1	13.6
Canada	100.0	81.1	10.8	8.1
Latin America	100.0	91.5	1.6	6.9
Europe	100.0	77.2	1.0	21.8
Other areas	100.0	93.9	1.4	4.7

Source: 1962—*Survey of Current Business*. November 1965, p. 19; 1963–65— ibid., November 1966, p. 9.

Although complete data are not yet available, there seems to have been an increase since 1965 in U.S. firms manufacturing parts and assemblies abroad to be sold in U.S. domestic markets. Nevertheless, the relative importance of this activity does not yet support the argument that this is the major determinant of U.S. overseas investment. On the other hand, these low percentages do not mean that there is not a very real and severe impact on the U.S. worker of such shifts in production as do occur. The move to manufacture components and finished products in Japan, Italy, Korea, Hong Kong, etc., has surely been felt by certain sections of U.S. labor.

4. Imperialism and Crisis

BEFORE AN ACCOUNT of how these economic relationships have persisted beyond the decline of colonialism, there are two further areas of dispute about the new imperialism which have to be examined. These are the relation of imperialism to crisis and the role of the state.

We turn now to the first of these: imperialism as the capitalist way out of crisis. Whatever merit there may be to this approach, it can become confusing unless an attempt is made to sort out cause and effect. The depressions of the 1870s and 1880s, the agrarian disruptions as well as the industrial crises of those years, probably speeded up the birth of the new imperialism. But they themselves were not the cause of imperialism. If anything, both the severity of the economic disruptions and the imperialist policies are rooted in the same rapid transformations of the late nineteenth century.

The roots of imperialism go much deeper than any particular crisis or the reaction of any government to the crisis. They are to be found in the factors discussed above: the expansive drive of each advanced capitalist nation to operate on a world scale, the development of monopoly, and the national rivalries associated with the needs of advanced economies with monopolistic structures.

What economic crises frequently accomplish is to make ruling classes and governments acutely aware of the need for vigorous remedial action. They remind laggard governments of their "duty" and prod them into action. Just as the reality of the contradictions of capitalism reveal themselves more frankly during periods of stress, so the reactions of governments become more overt under such pressure. But the policies and practices of economic and political imperialism are as much part of prosperity as of depression. More energetic and farsighted governments will act, or prepare to act, in periods of calm and prosperity.

Timid and shortsighted governments will either wake up when the crisis hits them or be toppled by a tougher political group.

A corollary of the argument that imperialism was a way out of depression is the idea that capitalism will collapse as the area for imperialist expansion shrinks. This thesis is based on an unrealistic and rigid view of how capitalism works. Cutting off markets and sources of raw materials creates serious problems for capitalist enterprise but does not necessarily portend collapse.

It should hardly be necessary to point this out after the many years of experience during which sizable sections of the globe have removed themselves from the imperialist orbit. Yet oversimplified, mechanistic formulations seem to have a life of their own. It is important to understand the degrees of flexibility that exist in capitalist society and which make the system more durable than its opponents have often supposed. Biological organisms show the same quality: the closure of one heart artery may be compensated by the enlargement of another artery to take over its function. To be sure, these organic adjustments are not eternal and they often lead to other and greater complications. But a significant lesson to be learned from the history of capitalism is that great troubles do not lead to automatic collapse.

The post–World War II experience provides a good example of this flexibility. The enlargement of the U.S. military machine became a powerful support to the U.S. economy. In turn, the success achieved by the United States as the organizer of the world imperialist system on the verge of breaking down gave other advanced capitalisms an important boost, creating markets and enlarging international trade. This flexibility, however, is not limitless. Cracks in the most recent imperialist arrangements are clearly evident in the strains on the international money markets as well as in the mounting difficulties of the U.S. economy itself. Further shrinkage of imperialist territory will create more troubles: it might lead to a sharpening of the business cycle, prolonged depression, mass unemployment. Nevertheless, as we know from historical experience, these do not necessarily bring the downfall of the system. In the final analysis, the fate of capitalism will be settled only by vigorous classes within the society, and parties based on these classes, which have the will and ability to replace the existing system.

5. The Role of the Government

ANOTHER AREA OF DISPUTE over the meaning of imperialism concerns the role of government either as an initiator of imperialism or as a potential agent for the abolition of imperialism. Here there are two extremes: 1) those who see government as merely the direct servant of large corporations and banks, and 2) those who see government as an independent force that arbitrates conflicting interests and has wide freedom of choice in setting policy.

Neither of these views, in my opinion, is correct. The operations of government in a complex society result in the development of a political structure that takes on the character of a special division of society, with responsibilities and behavior problems adapted to maintaining political power. As such, a government may be more or less responsive to the needs of particular firms or industries. Aside from differences over tactics, the actions of governing groups will be influenced by previous political experience and training, as well as by their own sense of what is best suited to keep themselves in power. Even a political regime responsive to the pressures of a particular industry or firm will, if it is competent and has integrity, withstand such pressure in the overall and long-term interest of the class, or classes, it relies on to remain in power.

On the other hand, the degrees of freedom enjoyed by ruling groups are much more limited than liberals are inclined to believe. To retain power, political regimes must have a successful economy. They therefore must work to improve the economic and financial structure at hand, and cannot pursue idle fancies of the "what might be if" variety. The more farsighted and aggressive political regimes—those which understand the main dynamic levers of the economy—will foster the growth of the economic system: they will build roads, harbors, canals, railroads, a merchant marine, acquire colonies for the stimulation of commerce, struggle for control of sea lanes to protect their commerce, and aggressively expand their territory (as in the United States in the eighteenth and nineteenth centuries). The incompetent regimes, especially those hampered by too much internal conflict among different would-be ruling groups, will rule over a limping economy. As pointed out above, a government often learns what is needed to sustain and advance the economic underpinning of its society the hard way; reminded and spurred by internal depression and/or the forward push of competing nations.

The limited alternatives open to political regimes have become increasingly clear during the history of imperialism. Here we must keep in mind the two strategically significant developments that mark the birth of, or prepared the way for, the new imperialism: 1) The internal conflicts among competing vested interest groups within the Great Powers become resolved in favor of the needs of large-scale industry and the financiers of these industries. Three such examples may be noted: a) the compromise between the Northern industrialists and Southern Bourbons in the United States after the Civil War; b) the compromise between the landed aristocracy and large industrialists in Germany; and c) the emphasis of the Meiji Restoration on creating the conditions for the rise of large-scale, heavy industry in Japan. 2) The successful development of large-scale industry is associated with increasing concentration of power.

Once the structure of each society had been successfully adapted to the needs of the major centers of industry, the path of future economic development became fairly narrowly defined. A later government, even one not a party to the previous resolution of conflict, has to pursue the same path: a comfortable environment for the leading industrialists and bankers, an environment that would stretch over as much of the world as these interest groups needed to operate in. The decisions on how best to create this environment, nationally and internationally, are arrived at by political and military officials, influenced by the latter's ambitions and ideologies. However, the ultimate test of government competence—its ability to achieve its political and military aims—is a successful economy: no welfare scheme can replace full and steady employment, operating factories, and smoothly run finance. And that economic success, in turn, rests on the success of big business and big finance. The practices of the reform administration of Franklin Roosevelt offer a good illustration: the stress on foreign trade expansion as the way out of the crisis, and the outright deal with the "economic royalists" (the term used by President Roosevelt in his bitter diatribes against big business) when faced with the needs of war production. It is instructive also to learn from the practices of liberal and "socialist" regimes in capitalist societies. Not having the kind of specific commitments and longstanding ties with particular business interests that conservative parties do, they are often *more* effective in making necessary repairs to the structure of monopoly business. What they do *not* do is undertake reforms which run counter to the basic interests of big business.

6. Imperialism Without Colonies

IT WOULD BE WRONG to say that modern imperialism would have been possible without colonialism. And yet the end of colonialism by no means signifies the end of imperialism. The explanation of this seeming paradox is that colonialism, considered as the direct application of military and political force, was essential to reshape the social and economic institutions of many of the dependent countries to the needs of the metropolitan centers. Once this reshaping had been accomplished economic forces—the international price, marketing, and financial systems—were by themselves sufficient to perpetuate and indeed intensify the relationship of dominance and exploitation between mother country and colony. In these circumstances, the colony could be granted formal political independence without changing anything essential, and without interfering too seriously with the interests which had originally led to the conquest of the colony.

This is not to say that colonialism was abolished gratuitously. Revolutions, mass rebellions, and the threat of revolution, the fear of further enlargement of the socialist world, and the maneuvering of the United States to gain a presence in the colonial preserves of other empires, these all paved the way for the decline of colonialism after World War II. The important point, though, is that the requisite dissolution of the colonies was carried out in such a way as to preserve for the mother country as many of the advantages as possible, and to prevent social revolutions directed to real independence for the former colonies. As long as the socioeconomic underpinning for the continuation of the metropolitan-colony relationship could be maintained, there was still a fighting chance that the interests that had benefited most from colonial control would not be endangered.

These observations do not apply to all the relationships of dominance and dependence which characterize modern imperialism. Some independent countries already possessing suitable social and economic institutions have fallen directly under the economic domination of one of the stronger powers and have thus become dependencies without ever going through a colonial phase. Some of these economic dependencies may even have colonies of their own. Thus Portugal was for a long time a dependency of Britain, and the Portuguese Empire was in a real sense an empire within an empire. It is not surprising therefore that the history of imperialism shows a wide variety of forms and degrees of political dependency. Nor is it difficult to understand why, on the whole, the major aspects of the imperialist design should exist in the era of declining overt colonialism just as they existed in the period of outright colonialism, since the primary determinants of imperialism remain: 1) the monopoly structure of big business in the metropolises; 2) the imperative for these economic centers to grow and to control materials sources and markets; 3) the continuation of an international division of labor which serves the needs of the metropolitan centers; and 4) national rivalry among industrial powers for export and investment opportunities in each other's markets and over the rest of the world. To this has been added a new factor which generates fear in the advanced capitalist nations and makes the maintenance of the imperialist system more urgent than ever: the inroads made by the growth of socialist societies and the spread of national liberation movements which seek to remove their countries from the imperialist trade and investment network.

The decline of colonialism has, of course, presented real problems, some old and some new, for the imperialist centers:

1) How best to maintain the economic and financial dependence of subordinate nations, given the aroused expectations accompanying independence and the greater maneuverability available with political independence.

2) For the previous owners of colonies, how to maintain their preferred economic position and ward off the encroachment of rival powers.

3) For the United States, how to extend its influence and control over the privileged preserves of the former colonial powers.

The problem of maintaining economic dependency in the new environment since World War II has been complicated by the rivalry of the Soviet Union and by the straining at the leash by some of the new independent nations (the latter, in part due to the pressure of the masses and in part due to the new elite seeing an opportunity to get a bigger piece of the action). Despite these complications, which called for new tactics by the imperialist powers, the essential structure of economic dependency has persisted in the period of imperialism without colonies. It is not a simple matter to eradicate dependency relations that have ripened and become embedded over a long stretch of history, beginning with the days of mercantilism. In the several developmental stages of the trade and financial ties of the colonial and semicolonial economies, the economic structure of the latter became increasingly adapted to its role as an appendage of the metropolitan center. The composition of prices, the income distribution, and the allocation of resources evolved, with the aid of military power as well as the blind forces of the market, in such a way as to reproduce the dependency continuously.

This point needs special emphasis since economists are inclined to think of the price-and-market system as an *impartial* regulator of the economy, one that allocates resources in such a fashion as to achieve the maximum efficiency in their use. This, in turn, is based on the assumption that there is such a thing as an absolute, objective efficiency which is equally applicable to all places and at all times. In reality matters are very different. The allocation of resources is the result of many historic forces. To name only a few: wars; colonialism; the way states have exercised their fiscal and other powers; the manipulations (at different times) of influential merchants, industrialists, and financiers; the management of international financial arrangements. In due course, wages, prices, and trade relations become efficient tools for the *reproduction* of the *attained* allocation of economic resources. And in the case of the former colonial world, this means reproduction of the economic relations of dependency.

To become masters of their own destiny, these countries have to overhaul the existing international trade patterns and transform their industrial and financial structure. Short of such basic changes, the economic and financial framework remains, with or without colonies. Even vigorous protectionist policies, adopted by many of the semicolonies, have been unable to break the ties of dependency. True, to some extent, they did encourage development of domestic manufactures. But in many of the more profitable areas, foreign manufacturers opened up factories inside the tariff walls and thus actually expanded foreign economic influence.

The state of dependency is not supported and reproduced by the evolved market relations alone. It is also sustained by the dependent country's political and social power structure. In the most general terms, there are three constituents of the ruling class in these countries: large landowners, business groups whose affairs are interrelated with foreign business interests, and businessmen with few or no ties to the foreign business community.[10] While the nationalist spirit may pervade, more or less, all three of these groups, none of them has a strong motive to sponsor the kind of structural economic changes that would be required for an independent economy. The interests of the first two groups listed above would be severely impaired by decisive moves for independence. The one group that could visualize a gain from economic independence would be the native capitalists, that is, those whose prosperity does not depend on foreign ties and for whom new opportunities would open up as a result of independence. But this group is usually small and weak and to succeed, it would have to break the grip of the other two sectors and destroy the economic base of the latter's power. Success in such a struggle would require an ability to keep power throughout the disruptions involved in the transformation; and it would depend on mobilizing the support of the workers and peasants, a hazardous undertaking in an era when the masses are seeking redress of their own grievances and when socialist revolution can quickly appear on the agenda.

Thus both the economic and political structures of the former colonies are well suited to the perpetuation of economic dependence along with political independence. And the needs of imperialism in the new situation could be met, except for one weakness: the instability of the power structure of the former colonies. This instability has its roots in the colonial system itself. In many colonies, the dominant power had in the past disrupted the traditional ruling groups and destroyed their political power. In addition, the mother countries created and sponsored elites which were psychologically and economically dependent on the foreign rulers. At the time, this was an effective and relatively inexpensive way to keep an annexed nation within the empire. Its weakness was that it prevented the emergence of the self-reliance and strength needed by any one sector to take power in its own name and reshape the economy for its own purposes. On top of this, the alliances that did develop to take over internal political rule were temporary and necessarily unstable. Finally, the changeover to political independence, especially in those countries where the masses were involved in the independence struggle, led to greater expectations of improvement in the conditions of life than could be met by weak postcolonial regimes. The people of the colonies identified colonialism not only with foreign despotism but also with exploitation by those who had adapted themselves to, and cooperated with, the colonial powers.

The retention of influence and control by the metropolitan centers in the postcolonial period has therefore required special attention. The techniques stressed, some old and some new, fell into several categories:

1) Where possible, formal economic and political arrangements to maintain former economic ties. These include preferential trade agreements and maintenance of currency blocs.

2) Manipulation and support of the local ruling groups with a view to keeping the special influence of the metropolitan centers and to preventing internal social revolution. Included here, in addition to CIA-type operations, are military assistance, training the officer corps, and economic aid for roads, airports and the like needed by the local military.

3) Establishing influence and control over the direction of economic development and, as much as possible, over government decisions affecting the allocation of resources. Under this heading fall bilateral economic aid arrangements and the policies and practices of the World Bank and the Interna-

tional Monetary Fund. These activities, in addition to influencing the direction of economic development, tend to intensify the financial dependence of aid recipients on the metropolitan money markets.

Central to the period of imperialism without colonies is the new role of the United States. The disruption of other imperialist centers following World War II and the concomitant growth of strong revolutionary movements generated both the urgency for the United States to reestablish the stability of the imperialist system and the opportunity to make inroads for its own advantage. Perhaps the greatest gain accruing to the United States as a result of the economic disruption of the war and early postwar years was the triumph of the U.S. dollar as the dominant international currency and the establishment of New York as the main international banking center. Thus was created the financial mechanism for enlarging the economic base of U.S. business interests through expansion of exports and enlargement of capital investment and international banking both in the home bases of advanced capitalist nations and in the Third World.

In addition to using its new economic and financial strength, the United States stepped up its efforts to enter the preserves of the former colonial powers by 1) becoming the main provider of military and economic aid, and 2) constructing a global network of military bases and staging areas. The extensive system of military bases is designed to threaten the socialist countries and to prevent the breaking-off of components of the remaining imperialist system. By the same token, the U.S. global military presence (in conjunction with the military forces of its allies) and its predisposition to actively engage these forces (as in Vietnam) provides the substance of the political force which maintains the imperialist system in the absence of colonies.

5.   Militarism and Imperialism

PEACE REIGNS SUPREME in the realm of neoclassical economics. War, militarism, and the pacification of natives are treated as merely elements which disturb the harmonious equilibrium models which are to supply us with the universal truths about the allocation of scarce resources.

One of the distinguishing features of Marxist thought, on the other hand, is the conviction that economic processes must be understood as part of a social organism in which political force plays a leading role and in which war is at least as typical as peace. In this context, militarism and imperialism are seen as major determinants of the form and direction of technological change, of the allocation of resources within a country, and of the allocation of resources between countries (notably, between rich and poor countries). Accordingly, price and income relations, treated as the ultimate yardsticks of economic efficiency and social justice in neoclassical economics, are viewed, in the Marxist context, as evolutionary products of capitalist institutions in which political force and "pure" economics are intertwined. Rosa Luxemburg put the Marxist case this way:

> Bourgeois liberal theory takes into account only [one aspect of economic development]: the realm of "peaceful competition," the marvels of technology and pure commodity exchange; it separates it strictly from the other aspect: the realm of capital's blustering violence which is regarded as more or less incidental to foreign policy and quite independent of the economic sphere of capital.
>
> In reality, political power is nothing but a vehicle for the economic process. The conditions for the reproduction of capital provide the organic link between these two aspects of the accumulation of capital. The historical career of capitalism can be appreciated only by taking them together.[1]

The facts of U.S. history provide eloquent testimony to the accuracy of this diagnosis. Thus, Professor Quincy Wright, who directed a major study of war under the auspices of Chicago University, observed in 1942: "The United States, which has, perhaps somewhat unjustifiably, prided itself on its peacefulness, has had only twenty years during its entire history when its army or navy has not been in active operation some days, somewhere."[2]

Professor Wright identifies years of peace as those in which no action of any sort occurred. A more revealing picture is obtained if we measure months of war against months of peace and bring the information up to the present. Adding up the months during which U.S. military forces were engaged in action—starting from the Revolutionary War and including wars against the Indians, punitive expeditions to Latin America and Asia, as well as major wars—we find that the United States was engaged in warlike activity during three-fourths of its history, in 1,782 of the last 2,340 months.[3] In other words, on the average, there have been three full years in which our armed forces have been engaged in action for every full year of peace. This comparison does not indicate the full extent of the use of military power by the United States to enforce its will. For example, it does not include activities such as those formerly conducted by U.S. gunboats in a "constant patrol in the Yangtze River . . . from the mouth of the river up nearly 2,000 miles into the very heart of China."[4]

It should therefore come as no surprise to discover that war-related expenditures have constituted the dominant sector of the federal budget throughout our history. Omitting the years of World War II and the postwar period, where the record is so well known, a tabulation of federal expenditures by decade, from 1800 to 1939, for army, navy, veterans' compensation and pensions, and interest on the debt (prior to the New Deal federal debt incurred was primarily a result of war spending) shows that except for one decade, at least 54 percent of federal expenditures were for military activities or preparations during the decade or to meet obligations arising from previous military activity.[5] The one exception was the decade of the Great Depression (1930–1939) when the percentage dropped to somewhat below 40 percent. In seven of the fourteen decades the war-related share of the federal budget was 70 percent or more.

This almost continuous preoccupation with military affairs was clearly not inspired by fears of invading barbarians. Of course, the competing colonial and commercial interests of France, England, Spain, and Russia were part of the reality in which the infant and adolescent United States had to operate. At times, self-defense had to be considered. Moreover, resolution of internal tensions, as in the Civil War, exercised a major influence on military aspects of U.S. life. All of this, however, occurred within a context of empire-building. For there has been a continuous thread in U.S. history, beginning with colonial and revolutionary days, of economic, political, and military expansionism directed towards the creation and growth of an American empire. The original expansionism, for which military investment was needed, concentrated on three main thrusts: 1) consolidation of a transcontinental nation; 2) obtaining control of the Caribbean area; and 3) achieving a major position in the Pacific Ocean.[6] It should be noted that this expansionism was not confined to what is now considered the continental territory of the United States: striving for control of the seas, as a shield and promoter of international commerce, has been an ingredient of U.S. policy from its earliest days. In fact, the struggle to incorporate the West Coast into the United States was, among other things, prompted by the desire to control Pacific Ocean ports for the Asian trade.[7]

The experience thus gained in the early stages of empire-building turned out to be most useful when the leading nations of the world entered the stage of imperialism. Several decisive and coinciding developments in the late nineteenth and early twentieth centuries mark off this new stage:

1) The onset of significant concentration of economic power in the hands of a relatively small number of industrial and financial giants in advanced nations. Competing interest-groups continued to exist, but now the success or failure of the advanced economies became closely identified with the prosperity of the new giant corporations whose modus operandi required control over international sources of supply and markets.

2) The decline of Great Britain's monopoly position as world trader and world banker. The burgeoning competitive industrial powers—notably, Germany, France, the United States, and Japan—pressed for a reshuffle of established trade relations and a redistribution of world markets.

3) Industrialization and new naval technology enabled competitive nations to build up their own naval strength to the point where Great Britain could no longer maintain unilateral control over the major sea lanes. As Quincy Wright put it in the study already referred to, "Naval inventions and the spread of industrialization had ended the *pax Britannica*."[8] Control over sea routes also involved establishing military bases where naval units could be refueled and repaired. The availability of decisive mobile military power

on the one hand required acquisition of strategic foreign territory to support bases, and on the other hand provided the means for aggressive pursuit of colonial possessions.

4) The earliest stage of the new imperialism engendered a race by the major powers for control of available foreign real estate. According to Theodore Ropp, after 1880 "every great power except Austria-Hungary . . . became involved in . . . active, conscious colonial expansionism."[9] Of the traditional colonial powers—the Netherlands, Portugal, Spain, Britain, France, and Russia—the last four continued to add to their holdings. (Spain, after losing Cuba and the Philippines, proceeded to conquer Spanish Morocco.) And, at the same time, five new powers entered the race for colonial territory: Germany, Italy, Belgium, Japan, and the United States. As for the United States, it was the Spanish-American War, of course, that placed it with both feet in the imperialist camp. And it was success in this war, plus the subsequent pacification of the Cuban and Philippine "natives," which satisfied two long-term U.S. expansionist ambitions: a leading position in the Caribbean, broadening the highway to the rest of Latin America, and a solid base in the Pacific for a greater stake in Asian affairs.

As far as the United States is concerned, there have been three distinct stages in the drive to empire: 1) the period when the United States was the supplier of food and raw materials to the rest of the world, when it was an importer of capital, and when maritime commercial interests were relatively very strong; 2) the period when the United States began to compete with other industrialized nations as an exporter of manufactured goods and an exporter of capital—a time when a small number of industrial and financial giants began to dominate the economic scene; and 3) the period when the United States becomes the major, dominant capitalist economy, the largest manufacturer, foreign investor, trader, the world's banker, and the dollar becomes the key international currency.

The energy and determination with which the expansionist strategy is pursued change from time to time. In the transition from one period to another, and because of internal as well as external conditions, it appears at times as if the United States is "isolationist" and uninterested in further extension of its influence and control.[10] Yet it is especially noteworthy that the drive for business opportunities on a world scale is ever present. Even when, as in New Deal days, domestic solutions were sought for crises, the development of foreign business was high on the agenda of government and private enterprise. Given the structure of the economy, the major operating levers work in such a way as to repeatedly reassert expansionism as the dominant strategy. In this perspective, the history of the years since the end of World War II is far from a new departure; instead, it is a culmination of long-term tendencies which profited by, and matured most readily in, the environment created by the course of the last major war.

The postwar leap forward in empire-building and the transition of U.S. society to rampant militarism are associated with two phenomena: 1) the desire to resist and repress socialist nations and to defeat national liberation movements designed to release underdeveloped countries from dependence on the imperialist network, and 2) the extension of U.S. power to fill "vacuums" created by the decline of Western European and Japanese influence in Asia, Africa, and Latin America.

Combating the rise of socialism is, of course, not a new objective. The destruction of the Russian Revolution was a top priority of the imperialist powers beginning in 1917. In this connection, Thorstein Veblen's observations on the Versailles Treaty in his 1920 review of Keynes's *The Economic Consequences of the Peace* are most pertinent:

> The events of the past months go to show that the central and most binding provision of the Treaty (and of the League) is an unrecorded clause by which the governments of the Great Powers are banded together for the suppression of Soviet Russia—unrecorded unless record of it is to be found somewhere among the secret archives of the League or of the Great Powers. Apart from this unacknowledged compact there appears to be nothing in the Treaty that has any character of stability or binding force. Of course, this compact for the reduction of Soviet Russia was not written into the text of the Treaty; it may rather be said to have been the parchment upon which the text was written.[11]

The failure of the United States to join the League of Nations reflected no slackness in its efforts to contain anti-imperialist revolutions: in Russia, these efforts took the form of armed intervention and support of anti-Bolshevik forces with food and other economic supplies; in Hungary, the manipulation of food supplies to help defeat the Bela Kun government. Surely the issue at that time was not fear of aggressive Russian or Hungarian militarism. Nor can much credit be given to political or religious idealism. The relevant motive, clearly, was recovery of territory lost to free enterprise and prevention of the spread of the contagious revolutionary disease to Western Europe and the colonies. Any such spread, it was recognized, would severely affect the stability and prosperity of the remaining capitalist nations.

Capitalism as an economic system was never confined to one nation. It was born, developed, and prospered as part of a world system. Karl Marx went so far as to claim, "The specific task of bourgeois society is the establishment of a world market, at least in outline, and of production based upon this world market."[12] One might add that it has been the specific task of imperialism to fill out this outline and establish a complex international network of trade, finance, and investment. Given this network, it follows that limitation of opportunity to trade and invest in one part of the world restricts to a greater or lesser extent the freedom of action of private enterprise in other parts of the world. The dimensions of the defense of free enterprise therefore become worldwide.

The United States had long ago accepted its destiny to open and keep open the door for trade and investment in other parts of the world. The obstacles were not only the heathens who wanted to be left alone, but the preference systems established in the colonies of the older nations. The decline of political colonialism and the weakness of the other great powers thus placed upon the United States a primary responsibility for the defense of the capitalist system and at the same time afforded golden opportunities to obtain special beachheads and open doors for U.S. enterprise.

With a task of this magnitude, it is little wonder that the United States now has a larger "peacetime" war machine, covering a greater part of the globe, than has any other nation in all of past history. Imperialism necessarily involves militarism. Indeed, they are twins that have fed on each other in the past, as they do now. Yet not even at the peak of the struggle for colonies did any of the imperialist powers, or combination of powers, maintain a war machine of such size and such dispersion as does the United States today. In 1937, when the arms race in preparation for World War II was already under way, the per capita military expenditure of all the great powers combined—the United States, the British Empire, France, Japan, Germany, Italy, and the Soviet Union—was $25. (Germany's per capita of $58.82 was then the largest.)[13] In 1968, the per capita military expenditure of the United States alone, in 1937 prices, was $132. This was only in part due to the Vietnam War: in 1964, our most recent "peace" year, the per capita military expenditure in 1937 prices was $103.[14]

One of the reasons for this huge increase in military outlays is no doubt the greater sophistication of weaponry. (By the same token, it is the advanced airplane and missile technology which makes feasible the U.S. globe-straddling military posture.) An additional reason, of course, is the military strength of the socialist camp. I would like to suggest a third reason: that a substantial portion of the huge military machine, including that of the Western European nations, is the price being paid to maintain the imperialist network of trade and investment in the absence of colonialism. The achievement of political independence by former colonies has stimulated internal class struggles in the new states for economic as well as political independence. Continuing the economic dependence of these nations on the metropolitan centers within the framework of political independence calls for, among other things, the worldwide dispersion of U.S. military forces and the direct military support of the local ruling classes.

Precise information on the dispersion of U.S. forces is kept an official secret. However, retired General David M. Shoup, former head of the Marine Corps, who should be in a position to make a realistic estimate, stated in a recent article in *The Atlantic*: "We maintain more than 1,517,000 Americans in uniform overseas in 119 countries. We have 8 treaties to help defend 48 nations if they ask us to or if we choose to intervene in their affairs."[15] The main substance of U.S. overseas power, aside from its present application in Vietnam, is spread out over 429 major and 2,972 minor military bases. These bases cover 4,000 square miles in 30 foreign countries, as well as Hawaii and Alaska.[16] Backing this up, and acting as a coordinator of the lesser imperialist powers and the Third World incorporated in the imperialist network, is a massive program of military assistance. According to a recent study,

> U.S. military aid . . . since 1946 has averaged more than $2 billion per year. It rose to as much as $5 billion in fiscal year (FY) 1952 and fell to as low as $831 million in FY 1956. The number of recipient countries rose from 14 in 1950 to a peak so far of 69 in 1963. In all, some 80 countries have received a total of $60 billion in American military aid since World War II. Except for 11 hard-core communist countries and certain nations tied closely to either Britain or France, very few nations have never received military aid of one kind or another from the United States.[17]

The above factual recital by no means exhausts the international functions of U.S. militarism. Space considerations permit no more than passing reference to 1) the active promotion of commercial armament sales abroad (contributing a sizable portion of the merchandise export surplus in recent years); 2) the extensive training of foreign military personnel; and 3) the use of economic-aid funds to train local police forces for "handling mob demonstrations and counterintel-ligence work."[18] These are, in the main, additional instruments for maintaining adherence and loyalty of the nonsocialist world to the free- enterprise system in general, and to the United States in particular.

The military forces of the politically independent underdeveloped countries frequently perform a very special function. This arises from the relative weak-nesses of the competitive elite power groups: large landowners, merchants, industrialists, and financiers—each with varying degrees of alliance to interest groups in the metropolitan center. When none of these ruling-class groups has the strength and resources to take the political reins in its hands and assert its hegemony over the others, the social order is operated by means of temporary and unstable alliances. Under such circumstances, and especially when the existing order is threatened by social revolution, the military organizations become increasingly important as a focal point for the power struggle within the ruling classes and/or as the organizer of political arrangements. Space limita-tions do not permit a review of this special role of militarism in the underdevel-oped world as, one might say, the skeletal framework of the imperialist system in the absence of colonies. It is this framework that is supported and nurtured by the practices mentioned above: military training and advisory services, the widespread military assistance programs, and the stimulus given to commercial sales of U.S. armaments.

This militarism which is working to control the rest of the world is at the same time helping to shape the nature of U.S. society. Some sense of the immensity of this impact can be obtained by noting the relevance of military spending on the employment/ unemployment situation. In the first three quarters of 1969, approx-imately 8.3 million persons were employed as a result of the military program: 3.5 million in the armed services, 1.3 million Defense Department civilian employees, and 3.5 million engaged in producing and moving the goods purchased for the military services.[19] At the same time, there are at least 3.7 million unemployed.[20]

Consider for a moment what it would mean if 8.3 million were not engaged in military affairs. Without substitute employment, this could mean a total of over 12 million unemployed, or a 14.3 percent rate of unemployment. The last time the United States had such a rate of unemployment was 1937. The per-centage of the labor force unemployed in 1931, the second full year of the Great Depression, was less than 2 points higher, 15.9 percent.[21]

So far we have not taken into account the multiplier effect. It has been esti-mated that for every $1 spent on national defense, another $1 to $1.40 of national product is stimulated.[22] If we accept only the lower estimate, and assume for the sake of the argument equivalent labor productivity in the military and civilian sectors, we reach a measure of unemployment in the neighborhood of 24.3 percent, in the absence of the military budget. Compare this with the unemployment rate of 24.9 percent at the depth of the depression in 1932.

A counter argument can, of course, be made to these broad generalizations. Unemployment insurance, for example, would to a limited extent, and for a very limited time, act as an offset. Conceivably, a sharp decline in military spending, if there were no financial collapse accompanying it, would reduce interest rates and thus perhaps stimulate construction and some types of state and municipal investment. A reduction in taxes would generate consumer demand. A rise in the federal social welfare program would have its effect. But it is by no means obvious that these counteractions would have anywhere near the same impact on the economy as defense spending.

Economists are to a large measure captives of the neat models they create, and they consequently ignore strategic dynamic elements which keep the economy going. For example, they tend to underestimate, if not ignore, the special effects of persistent inflation on business practices regarding inventory accumulation and investment in plant and equipment. Even more important is the almost total neglect of the influence of stock market and real estate speculation on 1) business investment decisions, and 2) the buoyancy of the especially important luxury trades. Inflation and speculation—partners of militarism— have been key triggers of our post war prosperity, and they are too easily ignored as economists blandly transfer a block of GNP from one category to another, as if such transfers are made in the economy as simply as one keeps accounts.

The experience of the last depression still remains a challenge to economists to come up with an explanation of the way in which the economy operates in reality. For example, consider where we stood in 1939 after ten years of depression. Personal consumption expenditures had finally climbed to a new high—6 percent above 1929 in constant prices. Yet, at the same time, nonresidential fixed investment expenditures were 42 percent below the level of 1929, and residential construction was 20 percent below.[23] Despite six years of rising consumer spending, and the start of orders flowing in from France and England for rearming, the investment community was still in a state of depression, and over 17 percent of the labor force was unemployed.

In this connection, it is important to recognize that one of the major attributes of the huge military spending in the postwar years is its concentration in the producers' durable field and the stimulation it gives to the demand for machinery and equipment. If we combine the spending for producers' durable goods resulting from the military with private spending for the same type of goods, we find the following: 36 percent of the output of the producers' durable goods industries is purchased directly or indirectly by the federal government.[24] (These data are for 1963, before the impact of the Vietnam War.) It is here, I suggest, that we find the unique role of military spending in raising and sustaining production and employment at new highs.

There are, to be sure, other impacts of defense spending that help to explain the magnitude and structure of the postwar economy: the unique role of research stimulated and financed by military and space programs; the special place of defense spending in nurturing the growth and prosperity of key giant industrial and financial enterprises; the support given by U.S. military power to acceptance of the U.S. dollar as an international currency;[25] the ease with which military orders can be fed into the economy in spurts which act as adrenalin injections to the private sector.

At the least, it can be concluded, economic theory and analysis which omit imperialism and militarism from their underlying paradigm are far removed from the reality of today's world. More realistically, it can be said that they operate to obscure the truth about the great problems and dangers of the second half of the twentieth century.

6.

The Limits of International
Economic Reform

EVEN THE BEST OF REFORM MOVEMENTS tend to foster illusions. And
the proposed New International Economic Order is no exception. Justifiably
dissatisfied with the traditional international economic order and the practices
of the imperialist powers, the leaders of the Third World have been energetically pressuring for a New Deal—one which its advocates hope and expect will
eventually result in a more equitable distribution of wealth between rich and
poor countries. The very unification of Third World nations around a common
program—and especially one that recognizes a basic conflict of interest between
the center and periphery—is undoubtedly an important step forward and may
even mark the beginning of a new phase in the history of imperialism. At the
same time, the rationalization and rhetoric advanced in promoting the program
raise false hopes about what can in fact be accomplished within the framework
of the imperialist system.

The ideas incorporated in the slogan of a New International Economic
Order took shape over a roughly twenty-year period of political struggle by
Third World nations to overcome what appeared to them to be the most obvious obstacles to their economic growth. It did not take long for the newly decol-
onized nations to become aware that political independence did not automatically remove the shackles of imperialism. And in one way or another they,
together with the older politically independent nations of the periphery, have
been seeking ways to unite and exert pressure for the redress of their grievances.

The first such move took place in 1955, when 29 nations sent representatives
to the Asian-African Conference held in Bandung, Indonesia. There, among
other matters, the participants raised one of the key demands for the economic

self-defense of the periphery, calling for measures that would eliminate the wide fluctuations in income derived from the export of primary products to metropolitan centers. The significance of that conference, however, went far beyond the drafting of specific proposals for reform, for it was there that the principle of the unity of Third World interests in opposition to those of the imperialist centers began to emerge. This conference was, in effect, a prelude to various other attempts to establish a political, and eventually economic, power base that would act independently of, and wrest concessions from, the metropoles.

Additional demands for changes in the existing international political and economic arrangements were generated at several heads-of-state summit conferences of "Non- Aligned Powers," starting with an initial meeting at Belgrade in 1961. Furthermore, the four United Nations Conferences on Trade and Development, beginning with the UNCTAD I gathering in Geneva in 1964, became important forums (and only forums) at which Third World representatives (2,000 delegates from 139 countries attended UNCTAD IV) spelled out their grievances and formulated demands for changes in imperialist practices in a selected number of areas on which a consensus could be reached.

While all these assorted activities fostered an increasingly clear and more integrated Third World ideology, they also intensified the sense of frustration. Meaningful concessions from the imperialist centers simply were not forthcoming, despite all the sound and fury, and despite the potential political power of a united Third World bloc. For all intents and purposes the metropoles turned a deaf ear to the demands of the periphery.

Two developments, however, forced the rulers of the imperialist centers at least to sit up, listen, and pay lip service to the need for reforms. The first of these was OPEC's success in achieving a major hike in oil prices in 1973. And the second was the change in voting strength at the United Nations. By the early 1970s, the number of Third World members of the UN had expanded to over 110. This voting bloc—supported by the USSR, Eastern European countries, the People's Republic of China, and Scandinavian countries—could constitute a majority on many subjects of interest to the Third World. No longer able to fob off consideration of the demands for reform to subordinate debating forums, the UN General Assembly itself finally acted on the matter. The 1974 Sixth Special Session of the UN General Assembly adopted a *Declaration and Programme of Action on the Establishment of a New Economic Order*, which was designed to "work *urgently* for the establishment of a new international economic order . . . which shall correct inequalities, redress existing injustices, and make it possible to eliminate the widening gap between the developed and developing countries. . . ." This was followed by formal acceptance of a *Charter of Economic Rights and Duties of States*.[1]

Yet, despite the vigorous program of action called for by these documents, the four years since their adoption have produced little in addition to still more conferences and ceaseless controversy on how to put the UN's resolutions into practice. The reason for this is simple enough. Each of the major items on the agenda—reduction of barriers to imports of manufactured goods from the underdeveloped countries, stabilization of income from exports of primary commodities, greater control by recipients over the transfer of technology, and debt relief (including, when necessary, debt moratoriums)—ultimately impinges on the profits accruing to the advanced capitalist nations. Not surprisingly, therefore, the imperialist centers, forced to enter into negotiations, have been playing a game of sabotage that takes one of two forms: 1) outright refusal to institute the proposed reforms, and 2) advocacy of counterproposals that either are mere window-dressing or are designed to meet their own needs, such as obtaining more secure flows of raw materials from the Third World.

These difficulties do not seem to have seriously disheartened the leaders of the periphery. For them the hoped-for New International Economic Order remains the reigning ideology and the focal point of their collective efforts on the international scene. And here it is important to recognize that the persistence of the vision, in face of the meager results which have been achieved, is itself a reflection of the imperialist snare in which they are perforce caught. This entrapment, in ideology as well as in fact, is rooted in the great extent to which their economic survival, not to mention progress, depends on the prosperity of the metropoles, or, to put it more concretely, on how much of their exports the metropoles will buy. This crucial reliance on external demand holds true even for those Third World countries that have adopted the boldest internal-reform measures, including extensive state intervention in investment decisions. It follows that in the absence of a strategy aimed to burst asunder the traditional mold imposed by the long history of capitalism, the peripheral nations remain, willy-nilly, cogs in the imperialist machine. And regardless of how aware they are of the constraints imposed by the imperialist ties, they are confined to bargaining for concessions, no matter how dim the prospects of success.

Those who have faith in the feasibility and efficacy of a New International Economic Order naturally reject this point of view. They are convinced that the removal of some of the external obstacles to growth will at least open the door to the development of self-reliant, independent capitalist economies resembling those of the advanced capitalist nations. At the heart of this position is the theoretical perspective, openly stated or tacitly assumed, that there are clear-cut, universal laws of capitalist evolution that apply equally to *any* country that chooses the capitalist road.

Now it is true that one can make a meaningful abstraction of evolutionary stages through which the advanced capitalisms of Western Europe, the United States, and Japan have advanced. Examination of this evolution, however, reveals that the conditions which have been basic to the achievement of these successful capitalisms are diametrically *opposite* to those of the peripheral countries today. And it is precisely these differences that raise serious doubts about the ability of the peripheral countries to duplicate in any meaningful way the evolutionary stages of the developed, self-reliant nations.

A full analysis of these differences cannot be undertaken here. Those interested in pursuing this theme would do well to consult Samir Amin's *Unequal Development* (Monthly Review Press, 1976) and his article "Self-Reliance and the New International Economic Order" (MR, July-August 1977). For present purposes we will merely note some of the key features of the developed capitalist nations that are most relevant in highlighting the contrast between the core and the periphery.

1) The industrial revolution, in the countries of its origin, was *preceded* by an agricultural revolution. Traditional low and unreliable yields of food and raw materials had for many centuries severely circumscribed the possibilities of economic growth. It was only after widespread and fairly rapid advances in agricultural practices enlarged the surplus of food produced in Western Europe that the threat of periodic famines was overcome, and therewith a roadblock to economic advance was removed and the conditions were created for an expanding market for both consumer goods and capital goods (initially primarily for agriculture).[2]

2) Typically, the spread of the industrial revolution involved extensive "borrowing" of technology. But the successful borrowers were those who did so mainly on their own terms, generating a large domestic supply of craftsmen and technicians. and actively participating in indigenous technological advances.

3) Continuous revolution in productive forces made possible persistent increases in productivity and an ever larger mass of surplus value, which in

turn gave a great impetus to the accumulation of capital and the growth of internal markets. The requirements of advanced technology and urbanization, among other factors, increased the value of labor power and hence set the stage for a rise in real wages. It is important to understand that although the exploitation of the Third World has been an essential component of the prosperity of the core countries and that export trade has been a crucial stimulus, the indispensable basis for the industrial growth of the successful capitalisms has been the ability to extend their *internal* markets.

4) Underlying the revolutionizing of the productive forces was the growth of a capacity to manufacture a wide range of capital goods as well as mass consumption goods. The development of a machine-building industry contributed a high degree of flexibility in coping with rapidly changing opportunities in internal and external markets; and the expansion of production-equipment industries was itself an important source of accelerating employment and hence consumer demand.

5) In each of the developed capitalisms an integrated and strong nation state evolved, one that was devoted primarily to the support of industrial capitalism and its allies in finance and trade. The state actively supported and assisted in the mobilization of internal resources for capital accumulation. Equally important, its foreign policy was instrumental in shaping the world capitalist system which became divided between, on the one hand, a small group of advanced capitalist countries and, on the other hand, a large number of peripheral countries subordinated to, and serving the needs of, the metropoles.

Now let us compare what has just been described with present-day conditions in the peripheral countries. There, for the most part, the agricultural revolution has still not taken place. Although high productivity has been attained in some export crops, the yield of most food crops remains incredibly low. As a result, the internal demand for more consumption goods remains relatively small: low agricultural productivity keeps a lid on farmers' ability to purchase industrial goods, and the small and unreliable surplus of food acts to depress real wages. Agricultural reforms, even those involving an honest redistribution of land, have not succeeded in removing the most important obstacles to agricultural growth. The reason for this is that the creation of a new class of small landowners by itself does little or nothing to mitigate the oppression of the farm population by larger landowners, merchants, and money-lenders.

In essence, what distinguishes the periphery's history to this day is that the engine of growth has been its exports to the metropoles. As a consequence, resources are allocated and infrastructure is constructed primarily in response to the demand emanating from the advanced capitalist countries, and only secondarily to that generated by internal markets. This type of economic growth does increase a certain kind of internal demand, but this is generally for luxury goods bought by the middle and upper classes. The backwardness of agriculture, depressed wage levels, and the persistence of mass unemployment stunt the growth of the markets for mass consumer goods.

Against this background, the potentials for self-sustaining industrialization are necessarily restricted. This has been clearly demonstrated by the experience of those underdeveloped countries which have taken initial steps looking to the achievement of greater independence and self-reliance. These efforts have assumed the form which has come to be known as "import substitution," i.e., the establishment of a domestic manufacturing capacity to replace imported consumer goods. The limits of this strategy quickly became evident, in part because it did little to enlarge narrow internal markets. More importantly, reliance on imports and the resulting strains on the balance of payments were not significantly eased: intermediate components, capital equipment, and in some cases raw materials, had to be obtained abroad. More recently, the shortcomings of this strategy, together with continued difficulties associated with traditional exports, have led to an alternative program for development: concentration on manufacturing industries geared to exports. And here we come full circle, for it is precisely the barrier to the sales of such products in the developed countries that has been adding pressure to the campaign for a New International Economic Order.

An additional factor of outstanding significance in frustrating the various attempts by the periphery to industrialize is the extent to which success remains dependent on the import of finance and technology from the West. To a greater or lesser extent, the Third World nations have failed to generate a population of craftspeople and technicians of the sort that enabled the developed countries to become masters of their own industrial revolution.[3] Nor have the Third World countries been able to create an indigenous capital-goods sector of a kind that would complement mass consumer-goods industries; in the few cases where progress has been made in machine-building, it has been confined to facilitating the manufacture of non-essential luxury goods and military equipment.

Finally, the peripheral countries—unlike the metropoles—have not succeeded in developing states that are single-mindedly devoted to developing and supporting a native independent capitalism. In general, the ruling power in these countries consists of class alliances in which groups tied to foreign investment activities are prominently represented. But even when the influence of the latter is absent from the top, the underlying dependency relationships tend to reassert themselves. For as long as the essentials of the traditional economic structure remain in force and the instability- producing influences prevail, the options for basic change are strictly limited. Any one of the recurrent crises inherent in the export-oriented economies—a critical balance-of- payments problem, a crop failure, inability to settle outstanding foreign debt—brings even the most independence-striving and determinedly reformist ruling group back into the dependency fold, seeking relief through more foreign investment or new sources of borrowing abroad.

If one examines the proposed New International Economic Order in the light of these considerations, it is clear that the reforms which it embodies skirt the major issues. This can be seen in each of the four key areas under consideration.

1) *Agriculture*. The advocated changes are concerned primarily with stabilizing and, where feasible, raising the income derived from agricultural (and mineral) exports. Wide fluctuations in income and adverse terms of trade do of course create serious problems for the periphery. But it is important to recognize that these proposals have nothing to do with the more fundamental constraints in the field of agriculture, which arise from inferior productivity in food crops and internal social obstacles to the expansion of the food supply.

2) *Exports of manufactures*. The main emphasis here is on the removal of trade barriers and obtaining especially favorable opportunities to penetrate the markets of the industrialized countries. Such concessions, however, would not overcome the normal competitive forces operating inside these countries. To outsell the products of metropolitan industries, the manufacturers of the periphery would have to charge consistently lower prices, an advantage that could be maintained only by keeping wages down, thus blocking the development of internal markets for mass consumer goods.

3) *Technology transfer*. Proposed reforms under this heading have to do with improving the terms under which technology is obtained from multinational corporations. While such reforms, if obtained, might ease some of the balance-of-payment burdens, they do not attack the central issue of developing an independent technological base and an indigenous research

and development capability for the generation of technology adapted to their special needs. In the final analysis, the proposed reforms would still keep the underdeveloped countries in thrall to the multinational corporations and the technology of advanced capitalism.

4) *Debt reform.* This has to do with much-needed relief from the stranglehold of mounting foreign debt. But the various forms of relief considered, including moratoriums, deal only with surface phenomena and not with the conditions that create more or less permanent debt peonage. The debt problem arose long before the rise in oil prices; it is an age-old burden which synthesizes the whole pattern of dependency. Recurrent balance-of-payment deficits stem not only from the instability of income from exports, but more importantly from the perpetual and ever swelling outflow of funds to firms in the metropoles in payment for shipping, insurance, banking services, royalties on patents and trademarks, management fees, dividends, and interest. Important as debt relief may be in the current situation, it can only serve as a temporary palliative as long as the conditions that create the need for debt persist.

Thus far we have discussed the New International Economic Order from the angle of the Third World. But what about the advanced capitalist nations?

It is conceivable that the metropoles might in theory be inclined to make some concessions, especially those that would bring them certain long-run advantages, such as securing more reliable sources of raw materials, protecting their multinational firms from nationalization or confiscation, and building up junior partners prepared to help preserve capitalism in the Third World. These possible long-run advantages, however, are offset by real and compelling constraints in the short run. The imperialist powers have entered a new stage of stagnation.[4] The international money system is shaky. World trade has slowed down. Trade and currency competition among the leading powers has been intensifying. Every one of the industrialized countries is confronted with internal problems arising from persistent unemployment and weak industrial and financial sectors. These are hardly the conditions under which the imperialist powers are inclined to consider reforms that promise to intensify their internal contradictions.[5]

The greatest illusion permeating the arguments for the New International Economic Order is that a new division of income between the rich and poor nations in the capitalist world system can be achieved through diplomatic negotiations. The more realistic question that needs answering is entirely different:

Is self-reliant development in the Third World at all possible as long as these countries remain enmeshed in the imperialist network and the basic dependency relationship remains? At bottom, the true issue rests on the choice between reform under imperialism and a breakaway from imperialism. The changes advocated by the New International Economic Order, even if by some miracle they were adopted, would not overcome the impoverishment of the masses, backward agriculture, distorted industrial and economic structures subservient to the metropoles, illiteracy, inadequate education and health services, and all the other ills that beset these societies. Solutions for such problems can only arise from internal changes in class power leading to a revolutionary alteration of social priorities which elevate the interests of the masses to the paramount position.

General, your tank is a mighty machine.
It shatters the forest and crushes a hundred men.
But it has one defect:
It needs a driver.

BERTOLT BRECHT

Notes

CHAPTER 1

1   See his letter from Moscow of August 29, 1957, quoted in Paul M. Sweezy and Leo Huberman, ed., *Paul Baran (1910–1964): A Collective Portrait* (New York: Monthly Review Press, 1965), p. 55.

2   The powerful influence of these ideological preconceptions can be witnessed in the "opened-up" debate on economic issues in socialist countries. A frequent reaction to the distortions and abuses of central planning is the uncritical worship of the holy market as a cure-all.

3   *Annuario Estadistico de los Estados Unidos Mexicanos, 1960–1961* (Mexico: D.F., 1963), p. 30.

4   The existence of certain types of dependent economic relations based on privilege is not sufficient evidence to characterize a feudal or semi-feudal society, nor did the existence of slavery in the United States make the latter—or even the southern region of the United States—a slave society. Slavery in the United States was in effect a special feature of United States capitalism.

5   Paul A. Baran and Paul M. Sweezy, *Monopoly Capital: An Essay on the American Economic and Social Order* (New York: Monthly Review Press, 1966).

CHAPTER 2

1   F. H. Hinsley, ed., *The New Cambridge Modern History* (Cambridge: Cambridge University Press, 1962), vol. XI, pp. 2 3.

2   The discussion on technology is based on the following: Thorstein Veblen, *Absentee Ownership* (New York: B.W. Huebsch, 1923), Chapter X ("The Technology of Physics and Chemistry"); Geoffrey Barraclough, *An Introduction to Contemporary History* (Harmondsworth: Penguin, 1967); David S. Landes, "Technological Change and Development in Western Europe," in H. J. Habakkuk and M. Postan, eds., *The Cambridge Economic History of Europe* (Cambridge: Cambridge University Press,

1965), vol. VI, Part I; J. D. Bernal, *Science in History* (London: Watts, 1954); C. Singer, E. J. Holmyard, A. R. Hall, and Trevor J. Williams, eds., *A History of Technology* (Oxford: Clarendon Press, 1958), vol. V.

3 Abbott Payson Usher, "The Industrialization of Modern Britain," *Technology and Culture* (Spring 1960), pp. 119–20.

4 William Ashworth, *A Short History of the International Economy Since 1850* (London: Longman, 1962), p. 22.

5 Alfred D. Chandler, Jr., "The Beginnings of 'Big Business' in American History," *Business History Review* (Spring 1959), reprinted in Carl N. Degler, ed., *Pivotal Interpretations of American History* (New York: Harper and Row, 1966), vol. II, pp. 109–10.

6 Along with the growing role of the investment banker was the increased use of the stock market for industrial securities. Before 1880, the stock exchanges dealt almost exclusively in railroad and bank securities. Until the late 1880s industrial companies remained too small and too little known to speculators. It was not until 1890–93, at the start of the major concentration and merger drive, that industrial securities began to be listed on the stock exchange and to be traded by leading brokerage houses. See Thomas R. Navin and Marian V. Sears, "The Rise of a Market for Industrial Securities, 1887–1902," *Business History Review* (June 1955), pp. 105–38. See also Gabriel Kolko, *The Triumph of Conservatism* (New York: Free Press, 1963), Chapter 1.

7 Geoffrey Barraclough, op. cit., p. 54.

8 Based on A. J. Youngson, "The Opening Up of New Territories," in *The Cambridge Economic History of Europe* (Cambridge: Cambridge University Press, 1965), vol. VI, Part I.

9 *The New Cambridge Modern History* (Cambridge: Cambridge University Press, 1962), vol. XI, p. 5.

10 Ibid., p. 6.

11 A. J. Youngson, op. cit.

12 See note 9 above.

13 Ibid., p. 6. As an historical reference point for this commercial revolution, note that the Suez Canal and the first transcontinental railway in America are opened up in 1869.

14 "There was some diminution in the size of armies in the period of tranquility after 1815, but after 1870 there was, among the great powers, a steady growth in the size and cost of armies and navies." Quincy Wright, *A Study of War* (Chicago: University of Chicago Press, 1942), vol. I, p. 233. Per capita defense appropriations in 1880 in the United States were $1.03; in 1900, $2.53; in 1914, $3.20. Ibid., vol. I, p. 671.

15 For excellent historical studies of the development of imperialist patterns in American history, see William Appleman Williams, *The Contours of American History* (Cleveland: World Publishers, 1961), especially the section, "The Age of Corporation Capitalism"; Walter La Feber, *The New Empire: An Interpretation of American Expansion, 1860–1898* (Ithaca: Cornell University Press, 1963); and Thomas J.

McCormick, *China Market: America's Quest for Informal Empire, 1893–1901* (Chicago: Quadrangle Books, 1967).

16 Note that giant U.S. corporations learned early in the game the desirability of controlling their raw material supplies. Vertical integration, including control over the mining of their own raw materials, was characteristic of the giants in oil, fertilizer, steel, copper, paper, explosives, and other industries. See Alfred D. Chandler, op. cit.

17 When Lenin gives his explanation of the transformation from competition to monopoly, he notes: "Concentration has reached the point at which it is possible to make an approximate estimate of all sources of raw materials (for example, the iron ore deposits) of a country and even, as we shall see, of several countries, or of the whole world. Not only are such estimates made, but these sources are captured by gigantic monopolist combines." *Imperialism: The Highest Stage of Capitalism* (New York: International Publishers, 1939), p. 25. Later in the essay: "Finance capital is not only interested in the already known sources of raw materials; it is also interested in the potential sources of raw materials, because present-day technical development is extremely rapid, and because land which is useless today may be made fertile tomorrow if new methods are applied . . . and large amounts of capital are invested." Ibid., p. 83.

18 Mira Wilkins and Frank Ernest Hill, *American Business Abroad: Ford on Six Continents* (Detroit: Wayne State University Press, 1964), p. 1.

19 Matthew Simon and David E. Novack, "Some Dimensions of the American Commercial Invasion of Europe, 1871–1914: An Introductory Essay," *Journal of Economic History* (December 1964), Table 2.

20 Note also: "The composition of manufactured exports has been changing ceaselessly since 1879 in a fairly consistent direction—away from products of animal or vegetable origin and toward those of mineral origin. Among those of mineral origin, the trend has been away from commodities closely tied to the production of raw materials, such as petroleum products, to metal products, including machinery and vehicles; and within the metal products group the shift has been to the more complex machinery and vehicles." Robert E. Lipsey, *Price and Quantity Trends in the Foreign Trade of the United States* (Princeton: Princeton University Press, 1963), pp. 59–60.

21 Op. cit., p. 62.

22 It is customary to think of competition and monopoly as direct opposites. This is proper according to dictionary definitions. However, in Marxist literature, the terms competition and monopoly are used to designate different phases of capitalist society. In neither of these phases is there either pure competition or pure monopoly. Indeed, it is the essence of the theory of imperialism to recognize that competition exists within the monopoly phase. Competition is between giants of the same industry (within and outside the nation) and between industries (steel vs. aluminum vs. plastics, for example).

23 Thus, all the iron material for India's railroads was imported from England. Even in the United States, which had a growing iron industry, iron rails were imported from

England. South Wales iron masters took part of their payment for this iron in the form of bonds of the railroad companies.

24   *Korea, Determined Strides Forward,* The Chase Manhattan Bank, May, 1967, p. 3.

25   For a critique of the "surplus capital" abstraction and suggestions for more significant analysis of current developments, see Paul A. Baran and Paul M. Sweezy, "Notes on the Theory of Imperialism" in *Problems of Economic Dynamics and Planning: Essays in Honour of Michal Kalecki* (Oxford and New York: Pergamon Press, 1966). Reprinted in *Monthly Review* (March 1966).

26   It is one of the significant ironies of these times that the wave of protectionism followed on the heels of the widespread adoption of the international gold standard. "The agrarian crisis and the Great Depression of 1873–86 had shaken confidence in economic self-healing. From now onward the typical institutions of market economy could usually be introduced only if accompanied by protectionist measures, all the more so because since the late 1870s and early 1880s nations were forming themselves into organized units which were apt to suffer grievously from the dislocations involved in any sudden adjustment to the needs of foreign trade or foreign exchanges. The supreme vehicle of the expansion of market economy, the gold standard, was thus usually accompanied by the simultaneous introduction of the typical protectionist policies of the age such as social legislation and customs tariffs." Karl Polanyi, *The Great Transformation* (Boston: Beacon Press, 1957), p. 214.

27   For documentation and analysis see George W. F. Hallgarten, *Imperialismus Vor 1914* (Munich: C. H. Beck, 1951); and Herbert Feis, *Europe, The World's Banker, 1870–1914* (New York: Augustus M. Kelley, 1961).

28   On the question of uneven rate of development: "Thus, Great Britain stood in much the same relation to most of the regions of Europe around 1850 that Europe and the United States bore to the Orient and South America a half century later." L. H. Jenks, *The Migration of British Capital to 1875* (New York and London: A. A. Knopf, 1927), pp. 187–88.

29   Lenin, op cit., p. 85. It is noteworthy that Lenin specifically rejects the definition advocated by Karl Kautsky which confines imperialism to the acquisition of raw materials supplying colonies; that is, the attempt by industrialized capitalist countries to control and annex agrarian regions. He debates this point in terms of the conditions existing prior to and during World War I: "The characteristic feature of imperialism is precisely that it strives to annex not only agricultural regions, but even highly industrialized regions (German appetite for Belgium; French appetite for Lorraine), because 1) the fact that the world is already divided up obliges those contemplating a new division to reach out for any kind of territory, and 2) because an essential feature of imperialism is the rivalry between a number of great powers in the striving for hegemony, i.e., for the conquest of territory, not so much directly for themselves as to weaken the adversary and undermine his hegemony. (Belgium is

chiefly necessary to Germany as a base for operations against England; England needs Baghdad as a base for operations against Germany, etc.)" Ibid., pp. 91–92.

30 We are referring here naturally to the main drift. France's attempt to break out of the close ties of the U.S. international system is one example of strain. Another example of potential strain is the program of important groups in West Germany to create a true political bloc in Europe which, on the one hand, can compete more effectively with the U.S. and, on the other hand, can be used to pull back some of Eastern European socialist countries (notably East Germany—but others as well) into their own imperialist "associations." These tensions are involved in the maneuvering with respect to the international gold exchange and dollar system, which will be discussed later in the article.

31 This and the preceding quotes are from Department of State Bulletin, May 10, 1965, p. 695.

32 The Economist, January 27, 1968.

33 For the background information on this, see Robert Engler, The Politics of Oil (New York: Macmillan, 1961); and Harvey O'Connor, The Empire of Oil (New York: Monthly Review Press, 1955). The clearest demonstration of the role of politics is found in the acquisition by the United States of oil reserves in Iran after the CIA-directed overturn of Prime Minister Mossadegh. Before the nationalization by Mossadegh of the British-owned Anglo-Iranian Company, U.S. firms could not break through this British preserve. After the overturn, five U.S. firms—Standard of New Jersey, Socony, Standard of California, Texaco, and Gulf—obtained 40 percent of the oil interest previously held by Anglo-Iranian. For the details on this, see Chapter 8, "The Blending of Public and Private Abroad," in the above-mentioned book by Engler, and Chapter 31, "The Threat from Iran," in O'Connor's book.

34 Same as fn. 31, p. 700.

35 Hans H. Landsberg, Natural Resources for U.S. Growth (Baltimore: Johns Hopkins Press, 1964), p. 206.

36 The Commission on Foreign Economic Policy, Staff Papers Presented to the Commission, Washington, D.C., February, 1954, p. 224.

37 International Development Advisory Board, Partners in Progress, Washington, D.C., March, 1951, p. 46.

38 The President's Materials Policy Commission, Resources for Freedom, Washington, D.C., June, 1952, Vol. IV, The Promise of Technology, p. 11.

39 Address at the Gettysburg College Convocation, April 4, 1959, in Public Papers of the Presidents of the United States, Dwight D. Eisenhower 1959, Washington, D.C., 1960, p. 314.

40 Rockefeller Brothers Fund, Foreign Economic Policy for the Twentieth Century (Garden City: Doubleday, 1958), p. 11 for the first item, p. 16 for the second.

41 Subcommittee on Foreign Economic Policy of the Joint Economic Committee,

Congress of the United States, 84th Congress, 2nd Session, *Hearings*, December 10, 12, and 13, 1956, pp. 127, 131.

42 Leo Model, "The Politics of Private Foreign Investment," *Foreign Affairs* (July 1967), pp. 640–41.

43 A frequent explanation for the upsurge in U.S. investment in Europe is the attraction of the European Economic Community (Common Market). This is contradicted in an analysis by Anthony Scaperlanda: ". . . the general assumption that the E.E.C.'s creation would cause a reallocation of international investment is not supported by the empirical data. Instead, the non-E.E.C. area has either maintained or increased its share of United States direct investment in Western Europe." "The E.E.C. and U.S. Foreign Investment: Some Empirical Evidence," *Economic Journal* (March 1967), p. 26.

44 Christopher Layton, *Transatlantic Investment* (Boulogne-sur-Seine, France: Atlantic Institute, 1966), p. 18.

45 Ibid., p. 18.

CHAPTER 3

1 American Board of Commissioners for Foreign Missions, *32nd Annual Report* (1841), as quoted in Richard W. Van Alstyne, *The Rising American Empire* (Chicago: Quadrangle Books, 1965), p. 171. The latter, originally published in 1960 by Oxford University Press, New York, is highly recommended for a better understanding of the continuity of United States foreign policy. See also Charles A. Beard, *The Idea of National Interest*, reissued in 1966 by Quadrangle Paperbacks with new material; and Lloyd C. Gardner, *Economic Aspects of New Deal Diplomacy* (Madison: University of Wisconsin Press, 1964).

2 *Niles' National Register*, January 22, 1842, pp. 327–28.

3 Foreword to Samuel Lubell, *The Revolution in World Trade and American Economic Policy* (New York: Harper and Brothers, 1955), p. xl.

4 Rockefeller Brothers Fund, *International Security—The Military Aspect, Report of Panel II of the Special Studies Project* (Garden City: Doubleday, 1958), p. 24.

5 The full title reads, *The United States Navy as an Industrial Asset—What the Navy Has Done for Industry and Commerce*, written by the Office of Naval Intelligence, U.S. Navy, in October, 1922 and published in 1923 by the U.S. Government Printing Office, Washington, D.C. The following excerpt is typical: "In the Asiatic area a force of gunboats is kept on constant patrol in the Yangtse River. These boats are able to patrol from the mouth of the river up nearly 2,000 miles into the very heart of China. American businessmen have freely stated that should the United States withdraw this patrol they would have to leave at the same time. Our Navy not only protects our own citizens and their property, but is constantly protecting humanity in general and frequently actually engages the bands of bandits who infest this region" (p. 4).

6 Eugene R. Black, "The Domestic Dividends of Foreign Aid," *Columbia Journal of World Business*, vol. 1 (Fall 1965), p. 23.

7 Address by Assistant Commerce Secretary Andrew F. Brimmer at a meeting of the Tax Foundation, Inc., as reported in the *New York Times*, December 5, 1965.

8 Richard D. Robinson, International Business Policy (New York: Holt Rinehart and Winston, 1966), p. 220.

9 "Economic Considerations in Foreign Relations—An Interview with Alfred Wentworth" in *Political* 1:1 (July 1965), pp. 45–46.

10 *The Conference Board Record* 3:5 (May 1966), p. 28. See also Judd Polk, Irene W. Meister, and Lawrence A. Veit, *U.S. Production Abroad and the Balance of Payments: A Survey of Corporate Investment Experience* (New York: National Industrial Conference Board, 1966).

11 This total consists of a) cash receipts from farm marketing plus consumption of farm products in the farm household, b) value added in manufacturing industries, c) value of minerals production, and d) freight receipts.

12 The Department of Commerce estimates that $6.3 billion of exports was shipped to foreign affiliates of United States companies in 1964. Other sources of non- comparability arise from a) the estimated $168 billion includes sales of trade organizations, public utilities, and other non-commodity producers, and b) the data on sales of domestic manufactures are on a value-added basis while the sales of foreign affiliates are on a value-of-shipments basis. Conservative estimates of adjustments to obtain comparability reduce the $168 billion to $110 billion.

13 John D. Lockton, "Walking the International Tightrope," address at National Industrial Conference Board, May 21, 1965, published by General Electric Co., Schenectady, N.Y., 1965, pp. 4–5.

14 William T. R. Fox, "Military Representation Abroad," in The Representation of the United States Abroad, a report of The American Assembly, Graduate School of Business, Columbia University, New York, 1956, pp. 124–25.

15. Hearings, *Subcommittee on Antitrust and Monopoly of the Committee on the Judiciary*, U.S. Senate, 88th Congress, 2nd Session, Part I, Washington, D.C., 1964, p. 115.

16. *Background Material on Economic Aspects of Military Procurement and Supply: 1964*, Joint Economic Committee of Congress, Washington, D.C., 1964, p. 11.

17 A. George Gols, "Postwar U.S. Foreign Petroleum Investment," in Raymond F. Mikesell, ed., *U.S. Private and Government Investment Abroad* (Eugene: University of Oregon Books, 1962), p. 417.

18 Clarence B. Randall, *The Communist Challenge to American Business* (Boston: Little, Brown, 1959), p. 36.

19 Joseph Grunwald, "Resource Aspects of Latin American Development," in Marion Clawson, ed., *National Resources and International Development* (Baltimore: Johns Hopkins Press, 1964), p. 315.

20 These are summations of data presented for 1950 to 1960 in U.S. Department of
Commerce, Balance of Payments Statistical Supplement Revised Edition, Washington, D.C., 1963. The data for 1961 to 1965 appear in the review articles on foreign
investment in various issues of the Survey of Current Business from 1962 to 1966.
The first line in the text table represents net capital outflows of direct investment
from the United States. The second line is the sum of dividends, interest, and branch
profits, after foreign taxes, produced by direct investments abroad. It does not
include the earnings of corporate subsidiaries (as distinguished from branches)
which are retained abroad.

21 John H. Dunning, *American Investment in British Manufacturing Industry* (London: Allen and Unwin, 1958).

22 Speech by Fred J. Borch, President of General Electric Company, "Our Common
Cause in World Competition," before The Economic Club of New York, November
9, 1964, printed by General Electric Co., Schenectady, N.Y.

23 Speech by John D. Lockton, Treasurer of General Electric Company, "The Creative
Power of Profits," at Macalester College, St. Paul, Minn., April 22, 1964, printed by
General Electric Co., Schenectady, N.Y.

CHAPTER 4

1 Carlo M. Cipolla, *Guns, Sails and Empires: Technological Innovation and Early
Phases of European Expansion, 1400–1700* (New York: Pantheon, 1965), Epilogue.

2 Obviously, the immediate objectives in the acquisition of colonies were not uniform;
some colonies were pursued because of their strategic military value in building and
maintaining an empire, others were pursued to prevent the enlargement of competitive empires, etc. The common factor referred to is in the colonial experience itself.
Regardless of the planned or accidental features of the acquisition process, the
administration of the colonies (and the manipulation of the semicolonial areas) was
aimed at, or led to, the adaptation of the periphery areas to serve the economic
advantage of the metropolitan centers.

3 The analysis of the surplus question is well developed in Paul A. Baran and Paul M.
Sweezy, *Monopoly Capital* (New York: Monthly Review Press, 1966). A distinction
needs to be made, however, between the question posed by Baran and Sweezy and the
one we are examining here. In fact, they deal with the concept of "economic surplus"
and not "surplus capital." The term "economic surplus" does not necessarily imply
"too- muchness" of capital. It is simply a surplus over necessary costs of production;
whether any of it is also surplus in the sense of the theories which relate surplus capital to capital export is a totally different and even unrelated question. In *Monopoly
Capital,* Baran and Sweezy deal with the basic dynamics of investment and employment in relation to the stagnation-inducing tendencies of monopoly. They argue that

the export of capital does not offset the stagnation tendency since the income return-ing home is greater than the outflow of investment. Hence, the export of capital inten-sifies the surplus problem of investment outlets rather than alleviating it. It should be noted that Baran and Sweezy are dealing with the *effect* of capital export, not the *cause*. And, in dealing with the effect of this export, they do not attempt to analyze it in all its ramifications. They are concerned solely with its effect on the disposal of the economic surplus in the home country. This is quite a different question from the one we are posing: What is the cause of the rise in the export of capital?

4 On the interrelation between British capital export and export of goods, see A. G. Fold, "Overseas Lending and Internal Fluctuations, 1870–1914," and A. J. Brown, "Britain in the World Economy, 1820–1914," both in the *Yorkshire Bulletin of Eco-nomic and Social Research,* May 1965. On the question of capital surplus and/or scarcity, note the interesting observation by A. J. Brown in the above article:

Professor Tinbergen, in his remarkable econometric study of the United King-dom in this period (*Business Cycles in the United Kingdom, 1870–1914,* Amsterdam, 1951), finds a positive association between net capital exports and the short term interest rate, suggesting that money became scarce because it was lent abroad rather than that it was lent abroad because it was plentiful (p. 1).

5 *Business Abroad,* July 11, 1966, p. 3

6 It is difficult to untangle all the factors to get a more realistic picture. First, not all the equity capital represents the original investment; some of it is reinvested surplus. The *Business Abroad* observation would apply only to the original investment. Also, there is a counter tendency which leads to an understatement of U.S. investment. In some industries, especially in the extractive ones, firms have written off assets which are still being productively used.

7 Note the more recent growth of U.S. direct investments abroad despite government restriction on the outflow of investment capital to reduce the balance of-payments deficit. *Business Week* comments:

More important, though, is the growing ease with which U.S. companies can borrow abroad. This year . . . companies will finance 91 percent of their planned overseas spending from sources outside the U.S., up from 84 percent last year. . . . Financing abroad has become so easy, in fact, that the federal controls on dollar movements from the U.S. have been only a minor obstacle to foreign spending plans. (August 9, 1969, p. 38)

8 *Foreign Income Taxes Reported on Corporation Income Tax Returns* (Washington, D.C.: U.S. Treasury Department, 1969).

9 Stephen Hymer, "The Theory of Direct Investment," Ph.D. dissertation, Massachu-setts Institute of Technology, 1960, since published in book form as *The Interna-tional Operations of National Firms: A Study of Direct Foreign Investment* (Cam-bridge, Mass.: MIT Press, 1976).

10   This generalization is obviously too broad to be useful in the analysis of any specific
      country. The class and social composition of a given country will be much more
      complex than indicated by the three large groupings outlined in the text; special
      country-by- country analysis is required if the dynamics of any particular area are to
      be understood. Thus, in some countries, attention must be paid to the role of small
      landowners, rich peasants, and rural moneylenders and traders. Urban business
      groups are also frequently more stratified than indicated in the text, with
      insignificant distinctions between commercial and industrial interest groups, and
      within each of these categories, different degrees of dependence on the industrial
      and financial affairs of the metropolitan centers.

CHAPTER 5

1   Rosa Luxemburg, *The Accumulation of Capital* (New York: Monthly Review Press,
    1964), pp. 452–53.
2   Quincy Wright, *A Study of War*, vol. I (Chicago: University of Chicago Press, 1942), p. 236.
3   Calculated from list in Lawrence Dennis, *Operational Thinking for Survival* (Col-
    orado Springs: R. Myles, 1969), appendix II.
4   Office of Naval Intelligence, *The United States Navy as an Industrial Asset* (Wash-
    ington, D.C.: Government Printing Office, 1923), p. 4.
5   Calculated from data in *Historical Statistics of the United States, Colonial Times to
    1957* (Washington, D.C.: Government Printing Office, 1961), pp. 718–19.
6   Richard W. Van Alstyne, *The Rising American Empire* (New York: Norton, 1974).
7   Ibid., chap. 5, "Manifest Destiny and Empire, 1820–1870."
8   Quincy Wright, *A Study of War*, vol. I, p. 299.
9   Theodore Ropp, *War in the Modern World* (New York: Macmillan, 1962), p. 206.
10 The isolationism was usually more apparent than real. See William Appleman
    Williams, *The Tragedy of American Diplomacy*, 2nd ed. (New York: Dell, 1972),
    chap. 4, "The Legend of Isolationism."
11 Thorstein Veblen, "The Economic Consequences of the Peace," in *Essays in Our
    Changing Order* (New York: Kelley, 1934), p. 464.
12 In a letter from Marx to Engels, October 8, 1858, in Karl Marx and Friedrich Engels,
    Correspondence, 1846–1895 (New York: International Publishers, 1934), p. 117.
13 Quincy Wright, *A Study of War*, pp. 670–71.
14 The data on military expenditures are the purchases of goods and services for
    "national defense" and "space research and technology" as used in computing Gross
    National Product. The 1964 and 1968 data are reported in the *Survey of Current
    Business*, July 1968 and July 1969. The adjustment for price changes was made by
    using the implicit price deflators for federal purchases of goods and services, as given
    in the *Economic Report of the President*, January 1969.

15 General David M. Shoup, "The New American Militarism," *The Atlantic*, April 1969. The figure of 119 countries seems too large. General Shoup was probably including bases on island locations, which he counted as separate countries. Our guess is that U.S. armed forces to man bases, administer military assistance, and train foreign officers are located in seventy to eighty countries.

16 *New York Times*, April 9, 1969.

17 George Thayer, *The War Business: The International Trade in Armaments* (New York: Simon and Schuster, 1969), pp. 37–38. This is a summary of data presented in *Military Assistance Facts*, May 1, 1966, brought up-to-date through fiscal year 1968.

18 For 1), see ibid.; for 2), see John Dunn, *Military Aid and Military Elites: The Political Potential of American Training and Technical Assistance Programs*, unpublished Ph.D. dissertation, Princeton University, 1961; for 3), see Edwin Lieuwen, *The United States and the Challenge to Security in Latin America* (Columbus: Ohio State University Press, 1966), p. 16.

19 Data on armed services and Defense Department civilian employment from *Defense Indicators* (Bureau of the Census), November 1969. The estimate of the number employed by private industry for military production is based on Richard P. Oliver's study, "The Employment Effect of Defense Expenditures," *Monthly Labor Review*, September 1967. Mr. Oliver estimated 2.972 million employed in private industry in the fiscal year ending June 30, 1967, as a result of Defense Department expenditures. We brought this estimate up-to-date by 1) assuming no increase in productivity or major change in the composition of production since fiscal year 1967; 2) using the expenditure data for the first three quarters of 1969, 3) adding space research and technology and one-half of Atomic Energy Commission expenditures, both of which had been excluded in Mr. Oliver's estimates; and 4) adjusting for price increases in the last two years. The resulting figure of 3.5 million is therefore a broad estimate, but the margin of error is not such as in any way to invalidate our analysis.

20 Based on data in *Employment and Earnings* (Bureau of Labor Statistics), January to November 1969. The 3.7 million estimate represents the full-time unemployed plus the full-time equivalent of those who were working involuntarily less than a full week. This estimate does not take into account the unemployed who are not counted in the government survey.

21 *Economic Report of the President*, January 1969 (Washington, D.C.: Government Printing Office, 1969), p. 252.

22 U.S. Arms Control and Disarmament Agency, *Economic Impacts of Disarmament* (Washington, D.C.: Government Printing Office, 1962).

23 *Economic Report of the President*, January 1969, p. 228.

24 Calculated from tables in "Input-Output Structure of the U.S. Economy: 1963," *Survey of Current Business*, November 1969. The percent of direct and indirect output attributable to 1) gross private fixed capital formation, and 2) federal government

purchases were used. These percentages were applied to the gross output of each of the industries manufacturing durable goods. It is generally estimated that 85 percent of federal government purchases are for the military. The figure is probably higher for durable goods manufacturing industries alone.

25 Given the inadequate U.S. gold reserves, the U.S. dollar can serve as an international currency only as long as foreign banks are willing to keep dollar credit balances in the United States as a substitute for gold payments. It is interesting that former Under Secretary of the Treasury for Monetary Affairs Robert Roosa included the military strength of the United States as a factor in maintaining the present international monetary system: "Moreover, the political stability and enormous economic and military strength of the United States have also increased the desirability of keeping balances here rather than in any other country in the world" (Robert V. Roosa, *Monetary Reform for the World Economy* [Mystic, Ct.: Verry, 1965], p. 9).

CHAPTER 6

1. A valuable summary and analysis of this history can be found in Orlando Letelier and Michael Moffitt, *The New International Economic Order, Part 1* (Washington, D.C.: Transnational Institute, 1977).

2. See Paul Bairoch, "Agriculture and the Industrial Revolution, 1700–1914," in Carlo M. Cipolla, ed., *The Industrial Revolution* (London: Fontana/Collins, 1973).

3. Some of the Third World countries, like India and China, have a long history of fine craftsmanship. Much of this (though not all) was destroyed in the heyday of imperialist expansion, when they were inundated by cheap manufactured goods from the industrializing center. To start over again without first withdrawing from the imperialist framework has proved impossibly difficult.

4. See Paul M. Sweezy, "The Present Stage of the Global Crisis of Capitalism," *Monthly Review* (April 1978).

5. An interesting and illustrative clue to their attitudes is provided by the alarm expressed by the huge steel corporations here and abroad over the entrance into the world market of a relatively small amount of steel exports from some Third World countries. Equally noteworthy is the recent treaty between the United States and Mexico, in which the United States reduced tariffs on fruits, vegetables, and handicrafts—a group of products which in 1976 accounted for $63 million of Mexican exports to the United States. In return for this munificent gesture the United States insisted on, and obtained, trade concessions from Mexico on U.S. exports of evaporated and other milk, lard, canned fruit cocktail, electric motors, and other products! (See Clyde H. Farnsworth, "Mexico Makes Reverse Concessions in U.S. Trade Pact," *New York Times*, December 3, 1977.)

Index

A

Adams, John Quincy, 68
Africa, 84, 85, 98
agricultural revolution, 127, 128
agriculture, 130, 136n29
aluminum industry, 51

Amin, Samir, 127
Argentina, 13
armament sales, 120, 121
Asia, 84, 85, 94, 98. *See also* specific country
Asian-African Conference (1955),124–25

B

balance of payments, 89, 129, 141n7;
    debt and, 87, 130, 131
Bandung (Indonesia) Conference, 124–25
Baran, Paul, 20–34; on bourgeois
    economics, 24–28; on capitalism,
    23, 25, 28, 30–32; on economic surplus,
    30–32, 140n3; passion
    and objectivity of, 20, 21–22;
    as social critic, 22–24
Barraclough, Geoffrey, 39
Baruch, Bernard, 68
Belgium, 63, 87, 117
Bernal, J. D., 22

big business, 38–39, 43, 44, 108, 109. *See also*
    monopoly; multinational corporations
Black, Eugene R., 69
bourgeois economics, 24–28
bourgcoisie, 29–30
Brecht, Bertolt, 132
business, 16, 41, 48, 51–52, 102;
    foreign investment and, 69, 70, 117;
    military spending and, 77, 78, 80;
    profitability of, 81–82. *See also*
    big business; industry
Business Abroad (publication), 97, 141n6
Business Week Online, 16

C

Canada, 60, 62, 84, 104; US investment
    in, 85, 88, 98, 99, 104
Canning, George, 12
capital export, 92, 93–100, 141n3;
    capitalist expansion and, 93–94;
    by US, 58–65, 70–71, 95–100
capital flow, 101
capitalism, 15, 38, 43, 119; Baran on, 23,
    25, 28, 30–32; colonialism and, 91, 92;
    economic crises and, 106; expansion
    of, 93–94; imperialism and, 13, 14, 35,
    86; monopoly, 46, 93; stages of, 127
capital surplus, 14, 30–32, 93–100, 127
Chandler, Alfred D., Jr., 38–39
Chase Manhattan Bank, 44, 70
chemical processes, 37
China, 19n8, 68, 70, 115, 138n5
Christian principles, 68
class relations, 15, 27, 106, 120, 132.
    See also bourgeoisie; ruling class

Cold War, 15
colonialism, 13, 41–46, 108–10, 140n2;
    big business and, 43, 44, 108, 109;
    economic dependence and, 17, 45, 109,
    110–11; metropolitan relations and,
    91–92, 109, 110, 112
"Commitment of the Intellectual, The"
    (Baran), 21
communications satellite system, 49–50
Communism, 90
Communist bloc, 58. See also by country
competition, 14, 85, 102–3, 135n22
consumer goods, 78, 128, 129, 130
consumer spending, 122
corporations, 97, 116; global/multi-
    national, 14, 43, 50, 89–90;
    monopolistic, 14, 81, 82, 95, 135n17.
    See also business
Cuba, 27, 117
cultural imperialism, 49

D

debt, 87, 96, 130, 131
democracy, 68–69
dependence. See economic dependence

development. See economic development
direct investment, US, 60–61, 62, 65, 101,
    141n7. See also US foreign investment

E

economic crises/depression, 105–6, 115, 122
economic dependence, 17, 33, 45, 87, 109,
    110–11, 120. See also colonialism
economic development/growth, 31, 34,
    107, 112–13; change and, 23–24; in
    peripheral countries, 124, 129
economic imperialism, 67
economic independence, 29–30, 111–12,

127. See also economic dependence
economic power, 83, 84
economic reform. See New International
    Economic Order
economics, 16, 114, 122; bourgeois,
    24–28; foreign policy and, 69; raw
    materials and, 39–40; socialist,
    26–27, 33; stages of, 29

economy: market, 24–25; military spending and, 78, 80, 123; regulation of, 110
efficiency, in resource use, 50–51, 110
Eisenhower, Dwight D., 57, 86
electricity, industry and, 36–37
employment/unemployment, 121–22,
143n19–20
equity and debt, 96. See also debt
Europe, 10, 39, 57, 70, 94, 104; agricultural
surplus in, 127; colonialism and,

91–92; economic security of, 58;
US investment in, 62–63, 84–85, 88,
97, 98, 99, 138n43; US militarism and,
118, 120. *See also* specific country
European Economic Community
(Common Market), 89–90, 138n43
export markets, 42–43, 52, 73, 94; foreign
investment and, 87, 89; military
spending and, 77–82. *See also* capital
export; trade

F

feudalism, 29–30
financial institutions, 41, 45, 94–95, 112–13
Ford Motor Company, 42, 65
Foreign Affairs (journal), 62
foreign aid, 69
foreign economic involvement, 67,
70–72, 82
foreign investment, 43–45, 93–94, 117, 130.
See also US foreign investment
foreign markets, 42–43, 45, 70, 76, 78

foreign policy, 68, 69, 81, 128; corporate
interests and, 70, 82–83; of United
States, 9, 10, 47, 57, 67, 76
formal rule, 12, 13
Foster, John Bellamy, 9
Fox, William T. R., 77
France, 59, 60, 63, 64, 116
free enterprise, 69, 119, 121. *See* capitalism
free trade, 69. *See also* trade
free trade imperialism, 11–12, 13

G

Gallagher, John, 11–12, 13
General Electric Company, 76, 89
General Motors Corporation, 65, 89, 97
Germany, 59, 108, 116, 117; investment in,
60, 63, 64
global trade, 40–41. *See also* markets; trade
Goethe, Johann Wolfgang von, 21

government, 50, 79–80, 105–8
Great Britain, 41, 59, 63, 64, 89; capital
export from, 94, 95; declining hegemony
of, 14, 116; imperialism of, 9, 10, 11–12,
13, 19n8; Middle East oil and, 48, 49
Great Depression, 115
Gross National Product (GNP), 72, 77–78

H

Haass, Richard N., 9–10, 16–17
Higher Learning in America, The
(Veblen), 26

Hobson, John, 13, 19n8
Hungary, 118

I

Ignatieff, Michael, 10
"Imperial America" (Haass), 9–10
imperialism, 27, 31; American, 9, 10;
    capitalism and, 14; cultural, 49;
    economic dependence and, 33, 67;
    feudalism and, 29–30; free trade, 11–12,
    13. *See also* new imperialism
"Imperialism of Free Trade, The"
    (Gallagher and Robinson), 11–12
import substitution, 129. *See* export market
independence: economic, 29–30, 111–12,
    127; political, 33, 46, 120, 124
industrial chemistry, 37
industrialism, 39
industrialization, 30, 41, 87, 116, 129
industrialized countries, 58, 131. *See also*

specific country
Industrial Revolution, 92, 94, 127
industry, 42–43, 83–84, 86, 107–8;
    technology and, 35–38. *See also* specific
    industry
internal markets, 31, 128, 129, 130
international finance, 41, 45, 94–95, 112–13.
    See also capital export; investment
internationalism, 93
International Monetary Fund, 47, 112–13
investment, 50, 80, 89. *See also* direct
    investment; foreign investment
investment goods, 78
Iraq, invasion of, 16, 17
iron ore, 53–54, 101
Italy, 59, 117

J

Jalée, Pierre, 14
Japan, 10, 57, 58, 59, 70, 117; industry in,
    108, 116

jet engines, raw materials for, 56

K

Keynesian revolution, 25

Kissinger, Henry, 16

L

Latin America, 13, 27, 84, 87, 104; US
    investment in, 85, 88, 89, 97, 98, 99
League of Nations, 118

Lenin, Vladimir I., 13, 19n8, 43, 135n17,
    136n29; on imperialism, 14, 35, 45–46
Luxemburg, Rosa, 114

M

Magdoff, Harry, 14, 17, 18
manufactured goods, 59, 130, 135n20
manufacturing, 37, 83, 104–5; investment
  in, 61–63, 89, 101, 103; monopoly in,
  82, 83; profitability of, 81–82; US,
  72–76. *See also* industry
market economy, 24–25. *See also* capitalism
markets, 40–43, 93; foreign, 42–43, 45,
  76, 78; internal, 31, 128, 129, 130;
  monopoly and, 102; world, 40–41, 95,
  116. *See also* export markets
Marx, Karl, 119
Marxism, 12
Marxist theory, 13, 14, 15, 114. *See also*
  Baran, Paul
metropolitan-colony relations, 91–92, 109,

110, 112. *See also* colonialism
Mexico, 27, 144n5
middle class, 26. See also bourgeoisie
Middle East oil, 48–49. *See also* oil industry
militarism, 18, 114–23
military dictatorships, 69
military power, 91. *See also* US military
minerals industry, 52–54, 100, 101, 135n20
Mommsen, Wolfgang J., 12
monopoly: competition and, 14, 85,
  102–3, 135n22; corporate, 14, 81, 82, 95,
  135n17; foreign investment and, 82–90,
  101–5; raw materials supply and, 84–87
monopoly capitalism, 46, 93
multinational corporations, 14, 43, 50,
  89–90

N

national interests, 90
nationalism, 33, 93, 110, 111
national policy, 69–70
national security, 58, 68, 77
nation-building, 16–17
naval power, 69, 91, 116, 138n5
Netherlands, 60
new imperialism, 14, 35–65, 91–113; big
  business and, 38–39, 43, 44, 108, 109;
  capital export and, 58–65, 93–100;
  colonialism and, 41–46, 91–92, 108–10,

112; economic crises and, 105–6;
  features of, 46–50; government and,
  105–6, 106–8; industry and, 35–38,
  42–43; monopoly and, 46, 93, 101–5;
  raw materials and, 39–40, 50–58;
  technology and, 35–38, 49–50, 54
New International Economic Order,
  124–32; key issues in, 130–31;
  Third World and, 124–27, 129, 131–32
New York Times Magazine, 10

O

ocean transportation, 40
oil industry, 16, 37, 85, 100
oil reserves, 48–49, 137n33

oligopolistic firms, 103. *See also* big business
Opium War, 68

P

passion and objectivity, 20, 21–22
Patnaik, Prabhat, 11
peace, militarism and, 114, 115
petroleum industry. *See* oil industry
Philippines, 72, 117
Planck, Max, 34
political control, 84
Political Economy of Growth, The
    (Baran), 22, 27–28, 30
political independence, 17, 33, 46, 120, 124
political power, 107, 112. *See also* power
poor countries, 99. *See also* Third World;
    underdeveloped countries

Portugal, 109
power: concentration of, 102, 108;
    economic, 83, 84; hierarchy of, 18;
    political, 107, 112; structure of, 111, 112;
    surplus of, 9–12, 16
President's Materials Policy Commission,
    55–56, 57, 86
price-cutting, 102
productivity, 127, 128
profit, 81–82, 90, 96, 103; rate of, 92,
    100–101; US investment and, 74–76
protective tariffs, 43, 45, 93, 111, 136n26

R

railroads, 38, 39, 92, 94, 135n23
Randall, Clarence B., 87
raw materials, 39–40, 42, 50–58, 95,
    135n16–17; secure flow of, 14, 126; strate-
    gic supplies of, 54–58, 103; supplies of,
    84–87. *See also* specific materials
regime change, 16
research and development, 50, 89
Resources for Freedom (Materials Policy
    Commission report), 55–56, 57, 86
resource use, 50–51, 110, 114. *See also*
    raw materials

Robinson, Ronald, 11–12, 13
Rockefeller Brothers Fund, 57
Roosevelt, Franklin D., 108
Ropp, Theodore, 117
Rostow, Eugene V., 48
Rostow, W. W., 58
ruling class, 10, 105, 120, 121; power of,
    107, 111, 112, 130. *See also* class relations
Rusk, Dean, 47, 49–50
Russia, 118. *See also* Soviet Union
Russian Revolution, 46

S

science and technology, 35–36
shipbuilding, 40
Shoup, David M., 120
social development, 29
socialist countries, 47, 110, 120, 125.

See also specific country
socialist economic planning, 26–27, 33
social synthesis, 22–23
South Korea, 44
Soviet Union, 15, 110. *See also* Communism

Spanish-American War, 117
steel industry, 36, 40, 144n5
strategic materials, 54–58, 103
surplus capital, 14, 93–100, 140n3

surplus value, 30–32, 127
Sweden, 60
Sweezy, Paul M., 30, 140n3

T

tariffs, 43, 45, 93, 111, 136n23, 144n5
technology, 49–50, 54, 89; borrowing of,
    127, 130–31; industry and, 35–38
Theories of Imperialism (Mommsen), 12
Third World, 14, 113; international economic reform and, 124–27, 129, 131–32.
    See also underdeveloped nations
trade barriers, 43, 104. See also tariffs
trade relations, 91, 94, 119. See also markets
Truman, Harry S, 57, 86

U

underdeveloped countries, 58, 67, 84, 87,
    102; Baran's theory of, 25, 26, 28, 31;
    investment in, 44; militarism in, 121;
    raw materials and, 51, 55, 87, 88; self-
    reliance in, 129; US investment in, 89.
    See also Third World
United Kingdom, 59, 60. See also Great
    Britain
United Nations, 47, 125–26; Conference
    on Trade and Development (UNC-
    TAD), 125
United States, 15–18, 52–65; capital export
    by, 58–65, 70–71, 95–100; direct invest-
    ment by, 60–61, 62, 65, 101, 141n7;
    expansionism of, 116, 117–18; foreign
    policy of, 9, 10, 47, 57, 67, 76; govern-
    ment of, 50, 79–80; leadership of, 47–50;
    manufacturing in, 72–76; markets and,
    42–43, 70, 76; mineral needs of, 52–54;
    strategic material needs of, 54–58
United States, imperialism of, 9, 10.
    See also new imperialism
US Defense Department, 54
US Department of Commerce, 71, 139n12
US foreign economic activity, 72–76
US foreign investment, 67, 81, 95–100,
    138n34, 140n20; business interests and,
    69, 70, 117; capital export and, 58–65;
    direct, 83, 88, 96, 97–98, 101, 140n20;
    earnings from, 74–76; monopolistic
    practices and, 82–90, 101–5; national
    policy and, 69–70; raw material sup-
    plies, 84–87. See also capital export
US military, 106, 115–16, 118–23, 144n25;
    corporate monopoly and, 82–83;
    employment and, 121–22, 143nn19–20;
    navy, 69, 138n5; power of, 11, 16–17, 47,
    48; spending by, 77–82, 115, 121–23
US military bases, 86, 113, 117, 120
uranium deposits, 87

V

Veblen, Thorstein, 26, 35, 39, 118   Vietnam, 57, 70, 80, 119, 120
Versailles Treaty (1917), 118

W

wages, 44, 100–101, 104, 128   world markets, 40–41, 95, 116
War on Terrorism, 10, 16, 17   Wright, Quincy, 115, 116
World Bank, 47, 112